YOUR PERSONAL
RETIREMENT
MACHINE

YOUR PERSONAL RETIREMENT MACHINE

A Guide to Financial Freedom

RICHARD C. CELLA, III

Assisted by Brett Machtig

Published by Advantage, Charleston, South Carolina.
Member of Advantage Media Group.

ADVANTAGE is a registered trademark and the Advantage colophon is a trademark of Advantage Media Group, Inc.

Printed in the United States of America.

ISBN: 978-1-59932-680-1
LCCN: 2015954792

Advantage Media Group is proud to be a part of the Tree Neutral® program. Tree Neutral offsets the number of trees consumed in the production and printing of this book by taking proactive steps such as planting trees in direct proportion to the number of trees used to print books. To learn more about Tree Neutral, please visit www.treeneutral.com. To learn more about Advantage's commitment to being a responsible steward of the environment, please visit www.advantagefamily.com/green

Advantage Media Group is a publisher of business, self-improvement, and professional development books and online learning. We help entrepreneurs, business leaders, and professionals share their Stories, Passion, and Knowledge to help others Learn & Grow. Do you have a manuscript or book idea that you would like us to consider for publishing? Please visit advantagefamily.com or call 1.866.775.1696.

TABLE OF CONTENTS

PREFACE

THE RETIREMENT PARADIGM

There is a major change occurring in the landscape of retirement and retirement planning in the United States. Consider that we are beginning an unprecedented sociological shift as the first wave of the Baby Boomer generation is entering their retirement years. This new group of retirees will represent a whole new set of demands on our government systems, such as Social Security and Medicare, while simultaneously shifting investor sentiment for an estimated $7.6 trillion of wealth accumulated by the largest segment of our population.

The Baby Boomer generation is estimated to include 76 million people! As of 2015 this populace ranges in age from 51 through 69 and will likely experience significant changes in the way they view retirement, quality of life, and spending habits. Currently, Baby Boomers represent a huge spending wave in the US economy. This great group of spenders who helps support our economic growth may suddenly cut expenditures and decide to save more of their earnings to enable themselves to retire comfortably. Our economic trends may change simply by virtue of a shift in the type of goods and services Baby Boomers demand as they approach retirement. Undoubtedly, this will have a significant impact on certain industries, such as health care and related businesses. In short, our economy will change to reflect their needs.

There has been a paradigm shift in the way people view retirement. In fact, many like me consider the term "retirement" a misnomer, even a dirty word! Most Baby Boomers I see starting this new phase of life are doing it in a much different way than previous generations. Many will continue to work in a chosen field, and that field may be totally different from that of their working career. We've all heard how people are living longer. In 1970, the average life expectancy of a woman was 75.1 years, and men averaged 68.2 years.[1] In 2014, the average life expectancy increased to 76.4 years for men and 81.2 years for women. However, for those people who live to age 82, the average life expectancy becomes 89 years for men and 90.5 years for women, according to the US Social Security Administration.

Health, fitness, and diet are more on the minds of senior citizens than ever before. Staying active is well known to lend opportunity for improved health, reduced morbidity, and increased enjoyment of life. I like to refer to what was once called retirement as financial independence or *financial freedom*—the time when people can live the way they want and do the things they enjoy, without being concerned with earning money.

As this same 78 million people lick their wounds from the recent stock market volatility and plan to enjoy their financial independence, they will be looking for new investment strategies designed for a much different outcome than they have seen up until now. As of 2007, Baby Boomers owned one-third of the value of all US stocks, according to the US Department of State. Two-thirds of that, or 22 percent of the total stock market value, is owned by the wealthiest 10 percent of the Baby Boomer generation. Younger investors may be advised to take heed from their older and possibly wiser pre-retirees. The drive for growth may be stunted by the desire for income and

1 Source CDC/NCHS National Vital Statistics Systems

stability. The hunger for capital appreciation may be replaced by the comfort of holding true value and receiving dividends and interest.

Our economy may continue to suffer from a weak dollar, massive government debt, and a long but limited recovery. It has never been more important for investors to build wealth, protect it, and properly prepare themselves to be financially independent. It has never been more challenging for the average person to invest successfully for their retirement than it is today. Yet, there are opportunities before us that can make it easier than ever for the average person to create above average wealth.

While this change unfolds, there is a renaissance of the 401(k) plan, with new regulations to help plan participants manage their money and lower their investment expenses. More effective web-based technologies allow participants to monitor their progress toward their retirement goals. These upgrades will positively impact retirement plan participants and provide more effective tools for building wealth on a tax-favored basis. This new and improved 401(k) plan is coming to an employer near you in 2015 and beyond. 401(k) plan participants now have more tools at their disposal than ever before to use the tax law for their benefit, take advantage of investments that previously were available only to the rich, and truly diversify their retirement portfolio while keeping investment expenses to a minimum. In addition, the technology available on most 401(k) websites will enable participants to project the savings and investment return requirements to reach their goals for financial independence.

This book is designed to help investors build and amass wealth in their 401(k) plan through clear and simple explanations of your rights, sound investment strategies, and examples of how to reduce investment fees. I will show you step-by-step methods for building your personal retirement plan, coordinating that with your overall financial plan, and developing investment strategies for different economic circumstances. I will also show you how to take full advantage of the tax laws and the benefits that Uncle Sam offers you. You have rights, and you've exercised one of them by purchasing this book. A wise decision! Now, take control of your financial future.

In recent years, there have been many critics of the 401(k) plan, and from what I've read, the criticism appears to be based largely on general assumptions and faults in the products offered by certain vendors who sell these plans. While some of this criticism is accurate, the fault certainly isn't with the IRS code or the ERISA legislation that created 401(k) but rather with the lack of education of the consumer (employers sponsoring 401(k) plans) and plan participants. Recent legislation such as the Pension Protection Act of 2006 (effective 2007) and the most recent ERISA legislation (Section 408(b)(2)) have made significant progress in changing the direction of 401(k) plans for the better. In chapter 8, we discuss optimal 401(k) plan designs in detail, as well as the services, credentials, and products that plan sponsors should seek for their 401(k) plan.

In this book, I look at things from a utilitarian perspective in that I believe my recommendations will be in the best interest of all who use them, business owners and employees alike, without harming anyone in the process except those vendors whose products are over-loaded with hidden fees or whose investment options don't allow for true unencumbered diversification. The book is written with the understanding that not all of us will become a real estate mogul and be good friends with Donald Trump, and not all of us will write books or inherit or build large businesses. It is also written with the understanding that it is best to identify methods to create positive change and take full advantage of the circumstances in front of us.

This approach will give everyone an equal opportunity to play the game and find their own success. I believe the 401(k) plan offers that opportunity, and for most people it may be the single best way to create wealth. Let's look at how to identify the right choices in these plans and the right advice from those people who offer it.

CHAPTER 1

THE FOUR PILLARS OF FINANCIAL PLANNING

F or most Americans and people in the free world, there are several common milestones in our lives that have a significant impact on defining who we are, who our friends might be, who our children will become, and how we see the direction of our lives in the future. These milestones include:

- going to college or other forms of continuing education
- buying a home
- choosing a career
- choosing when to leave your career
- dying

If you were to look at your closest group of friends, most people would find that they're primarily made up of people they went to school or college with, people they work with, or their neighbors. The people closest to us influence so much of what makes us who we are and the beliefs we represent. Our friends and colleagues are the people we may be most influenced by and the people we may have the most influence on. Therefore, in many ways, the schools we attend, the neighborhood we live in, where we work, and the direction of our career shapes who we are. I am aware that we all are unique and have core values that belong to us alone. However, these external influences are indisputable.

Think of when you and your family were considering which home to buy. The first thing you likely decided was which community you wanted to live in. You probably thought of the type of neighborhood you wanted to live in and raise your children in and what type of school system they had as opposed to whether there were granite countertops in the kitchen or bathroom. Choosing where to live is an important life decision, and buying a home is a very substantial financial commitment. This one decision can have a very significant impact on your life and the lives of your children.

Continuing your education is an important commitment to improving your lifestyle and seeking to fulfill your goals and visions for the future. Likewise, by assisting your children to further their education, you enable them to constructively build their lives to seek fulfillment of their dreams and aspirations. Their decision to go to college or learn a trade, as well as their choice of schools, can have a profound influence on their life, their level of accomplishment, and their sphere of effect.

As we go through these phases of our life, we establish friendships and acquaintances that in some ways affect our direction and the decisions we make. This could be as simple as buying a particular car because one of our friends gave it rave reviews. We might choose anything—from the books we read to where we vacation—based on the comments or experiences of people we know. It could also be as significant as deciding how and where to spend our retirement years. For our children, their friends and acquaintances from school may help lead them to career opportunities that have a positive influence on their lives. So much of what we decide is at least partially influenced by the opinions and experiences of the people we trust. So it stands to reason that to some degree we also wish to seek similar levels of financial success or be driven to have similar lifestyles as our friends. It's natural that we would want to have these things in common with them or that we would want for them to share some of our own traits. We relate to our closest friends, and we want to feel as though we belong. Our vision of self is partially determined by our perception of how our friends see us.

By now, you're probably rechecking the title of this book and asking how this all relates to your financial planning. There are two important points of consideration here:

- First, it's clear that financial decisions and lifestyle decisions are interrelated. It's also human nature to have an element of keeping up with the Joneses in our buying decisions.

- Your plan to retire and declare financial independence must acknowledge that such a declaration will require you to have the ability to maintain a similar lifestyle in retirement to that which exists during your latest working years.

Making good decisions about your education and your career can strengthen and improve your financial position throughout your working life. However, your financial decisions, particularly regarding your most significant financial commitments, will determine your ultimate level of financial success. Therefore, the second important point to consider is that it is of paramount importance that we understand the following: *While there may be many emotions and feelings, such as pride, that will influence how we use our money, it is critical that we balance those emotional needs with our true long-term financial needs.*

The Four Pillars of Financial Planning are based on the four most critical financial matters in your life.

THESE FOUR PILLARS ARE:

1. buying a home

2. college education for yourself and your children

3. retirement or financial freedom

4. estate planning (for your heirs)

Sure, there may be many other critical financial decisions you'll have to make in your life but none that could have the potential to be more beneficial or damaging than those related to the Four Pillars. In this book, we focus on retirement planning, but instead of referring to "retirement," I refer to that American dream as *financial freedom.* I firmly believe that financial freedom is the single most important aspect of your financial planning. Why do I believe that retirement or financial freedom planning is the single most critical element of the Four Pillars of Financial Planning? It is the only one in which the effect of time is immediately recognized and is irreversible in virtually every case. *Of all the resources a person can acquire or have at their disposal, none is more valuable than time, and the less you have the more precious it becomes.* When it comes to financial freedom planning, time is just as precious. Each day that passes has a cost that can never be recovered.

Throughout this book, you will find a series of "Action Items" that provide our readers with a timely summary of steps that they can take to help build a successful retirement plan. You can follow these Action Items as you read the book or refer back to them later to guide you through the process of establishing your plans to achieve financial freedom. Later in this chapter, we take a closer look at the impact of timing and decisions related to the Four Pillars of Financial Planning to assist us in understanding their relative importance. In the meantime, please review the Action Items below and take action for yourself to achieve your personal financial goals.

ACTION ITEMS

Review your financial plan. Check to be sure it has been updated for changes in occupation, salary levels, children's education plans, family health issues, and your goals for financial freedom. Ask yourself what it would mean to have financial freedom.

If your response to this first Action Item is to say that you don't have a financial plan, run to the phone, call a financial advisor, and put together a well-thought-out financial plan as soon as possible! I don't gamble, but if I had to bet on something, I would bet that you will not achieve financial freedom without it.

HOME OWNERSHIP

You can always buy a house, even if you wished you had done so earlier in life. The financial impact of not doing so sooner may be irrelevant to your overall financial health. This is not to say that I don't believe in home ownership, I do, but not because I think it's going to make you wealthy! The essence of asset creation through home ownership results from the forced savings associated with your monthly payments and the fact that money spent on home improvements while providing you with gratification will often be largely returned in home equity. However, let's not mince words—your home is not an investment, it's an expense! Therefore, purchasing a home later rather than sooner, for whatever your reasons may be, will not have a significant impact on your overall financial health.

Home ownership can also be a dangerous trap for those of us who seek form over function. This is an area where "keeping up with the Joneses" can be costly. In short, *the greater the financial commitment, the more important it is that you stay within your financial means.*

I recently completed a calculation where I compared my monthly outlay, maintenance costs, and home improvement costs of my prior (smaller) home to my current home. I compared the home improvement costs of my new home to what the typical home improvements at my prior residence would have been. I factored in the mortgage payment difference net after tax (given tax treatment for interest). I also then factored in the cash I added to the net proceeds (equity) from the sale of my prior home to make the down payment on the new home. After nearly ten years of living in my current (larger) home, I determined that had I stayed in my old (smaller) house I would have accumulated approximately $201,000 additional liquid cash in my bank account plus interest! What's more disconcerting is that real estate values have actually gone down since 2003 when I bought the house, so I have no added equity to show for this additional expenditure.

In other words, by upgrading to a larger, more desirable home it has cost me over $20,000 per year in additional interest and home ownership costs. I can also say that my home ownership costs in my prior home were similar to the rental costs of a good quality upscale apartment. Therefore, it can also be said that had I chosen not to buy a home and rented a good quality apartment, I would have saved $20,000 per year!

EDUCATION

You can always further your education. I grant you that an investment in your education earlier in life can provide you with increased income opportunity. However, there is just as much opportunity to create wealth by collecting trash or laundering clothes as there is writing software or becoming president of a bank. It simply depends on your level of determination and commitment to that success. In my home state of Massachusetts, there is a very successful pizza business in which the founder and president never went to college, yet he has built a substantial organization whose products are sold in supermarkets and through wholesale channels, as well as through dozens of their pizza shops. Now that the business has become so successful, the owner has enrolled in Harvard Business School to further his business management skills so that he may more effectively manage and grow his company going forward.

The pizza company is one of many examples of how people with no more than a high school education have become highly successful in building a business. It's a common theme among successful business owners that they attribute their success to dogged determination, belief in themselves, strong team-building skills, and a dose of good fortune. The most valuable part of their education came from their experiences in the pursuit of success rather than the books they read in school.

As for your children's education, you can always help them through student loans, home equity loans, or even borrowing funds from your 401(k), so long as you've saved sufficiently beyond the minimum necessary to achieve your financial goals. I believe an investment in your children's education is wise and will pay off in many ways. To have their appreciation for your support and their recognition for helping them realize their dreams is invaluable. To see your children succeed is clearly one of the most gratifying aspects of family life, and money can't buy pride of this magnitude.

In the latter case, a 401(k) loan can be an attractive alternative should you have sufficient funds available. I would define "sufficient" as being on track or ahead of schedule with your long-term savings goals. When you take a loan from your 401(k), you will be required to make loan repayments, including interest, through payroll deduction. However, because you are borrowing from yourself (your own 401(k) investments), the interest you pay is credited back to your account. Therefore, the cost of such a loan is primarily the investment return opportunity lost by taking the money out of the 401(k) plan investment funds. The difficulty with borrowing from your 401(k) is that when it comes to repaying the loan, many people reduce or eliminate their new contributions due to the payroll deduction of the loan repayment. This can be very damaging to your long-term success, as we see later in this book. *Therefore, a 401(k) loan is only allowable if you can discipline yourself to continue with your regular 401(k) contri-*

butions while making the loan payments. In this case, a 401(k) loan will not have such a negative effect on your financial future.

For the record, I advise all of my clients with young children to save money in a 529 college savings plan. However, this must be done *after* they've met their savings objective for their financial freedom plan. The 529 plan offers several attractive tax benefits and long-term savings advantages. The essence of the 529 plan is that the investments grow tax deferred and will be considered tax exempt upon distribution if used to pay for college education. The additional benefits include the fact that the donor, usually the parents, keeps control of the assets and may change the beneficiary of the accounts at a future date. Should the child not go to college or receive significant scholarships, the money can be used to help another child or even be kept by the parents and saved on a tax-deferred basis to supplement their income during their financial freedom years (subject to taxation).

ESTATE PLANNING

There is surely an element of timing in estate planning that is important. However, so long as a person adequately insures their life and long-term health care, in many cases the most critical elements of estate planning can be done late in life or even after death if there's a surviving spouse. Estate planning becomes more complex for individuals and families with greater wealth, as their estates may be subject to estate taxes after death. Simply put, if you have not amassed wealth in excess of $5.3 million (per spouse if married), then you do not have much of a federal estate tax concern. This does not mean that you shouldn't engage in estate planning, just that the process of establishing a successful plan is simpler.

If you or your spouse have been divorced and remarried, and there are children from those previous marriages, then you require special estate planning that should be addressed immediately. The potential for financial deficiencies, discord, and hurt among family members after your death is quite real when you consider that there are often preexisting psychological barriers between children and their stepparents. Equally important is the protection of the surviving spouse from the potential loss of use of assets such as your residence, vacation property, or other assets that may be in the name of only one spouse. Many times the income of the surviving spouse is significantly less than that of the deceased, which would indicate the need for income protection for that spouse. This is particularly important if the deceased intended to pass his or her assets to their children at death. The absence of a will and/or a proper allocation of the family assets could result in an expensive and distressing legal battle, a surviving spouse with less than adequate resources, and possibly children of the deceased who are left with feelings of abandonment or dissatisfaction.

Everyone should establish a basic estate plan, including a revocable living trust, health care proxy, and "credit shelter trusts" for married couples. The credit shelter trust enables married couples to lock in the full benefit of the "unified estate tax credit" for both spouses while also taking advantage of the unlimited marital deduction. This process will enable most families to minimize or avoid federal estate taxes. Families of children with special needs should also consider establishing special needs trusts to protect those children's accumulated assets, life insurance benefits, and inheritances over time.

I suggest that estate planning is an extension of your love for your family as well as an extension of your ability to manage your affairs beyond your living years for the benefit of your family.

Consider it a matter of organizing your financial affairs in anticipation of not being there to manage them at some point in the future.

- How would you want things handled?

- What do you want your family members to have in your absence?

- From what financial circumstances would you want them to be protected?

The good news is that so long as you're alive, you'll have the opportunity to address these issues.

FINANCIAL FREEDOM PLANNING

Unlike the other pillars of financial planning, when it comes to planning for your financial freedom, each week that passes in which you've failed to save the appropriate funds for your freedom plan, you have suffered a loss that cannot be recovered. The time value of money is one of the greatest assets to a diligent saver and one of the harshest realities to someone who waited too long to prepare and save in earnest. The benefit of regular (weekly/monthly) savings is one of the key factors for someone of modest means to have the ability to create significant wealth. In the majority of cases, each month that passes without adequate savings represents a reduction in the total amount saved by age 60, 65, or 67. *The earliest dollars saved are the most valuable retirement income producers.*

ACTION ITEMS

If you own a home, review your current mortgage interest rate and determine if you can get a lower rate by refinancing. Shop interest rates with banks and mortgage companies to get the best terms.

If you have young children, consider opening a 529 college savings plan for at least your oldest child. Begin saving with regular monthly deposits of whatever amount you can afford without reducing your 401(k) contributions. Invest in an "age-based" balanced portfolio.

If you do not have an estate plan or a will, consider seeking the assistance of an attorney and establish a revocable living trust.

CHAPTER 2

THE FAMILY BUSINESS

O ver the last 30 years, I have helped thousands of people with various types of financial and investment advice and spent thousands of hours outlining and explaining how it all really works. Maybe the best tool I have in my skill set for helping people is my ability to put it all in terms that are simple to understand. I've learned to do that as a way of adapting to one of the most difficult challenges in my profession—overcoming the natural defense mechanisms people have about discussing their finances. Many people find the topic overwhelming or confusing and as a result put off establishing programs that may help them. Some people simply procrastinate in significant and detrimental fashion, and others feel threatened by what they don't understand. Still others may be afraid that they will lose freedom or control by committing to a (savings) plan. *All of these things could add up to a failure to achieve success in establishing sound financial strategies.*

So the first thing I explain to my clients is to look at their finances as a family business. The fact that becomes clear is that, as a family business, it should be operated with a tendency toward business strategy to achieve financial success. Let's look at some basic characteristics of a business:

> First: you want to have a product or service to sell, and you must believe there is a demand for that product or service such that you can make a profit selling it. You may also believe that your product is better than the competition's; therefore, you may be able to get paid more for yours than what other businesses get.

> Second: you will need certain resources, equipment, and transportation to facilitate the operation of your business.

> Third: you recognize that you'll need to spend only an amount of money on those resources that will allow you to have a net profit left over to keep when you're done. Sound about right?

You may borrow funds to invest in the development of your business (good debt) such as furthering education, buying more advanced technology systems, or buying better equipment to operate or transport your business. These are all worthy uses of debt that can help you be more efficient, increase your profitability, and build your business. Unfortunately, many small businesses fail due to inadequate cash reserves and excess debt from nonproductive expenditures (bad debt) such as unnecessary perks, large cash bonuses for key executives, or lavish trips paid for with credit cards when there's not enough cash in the bank to cover it. These types of expenditures and debt ultimately negate much if not all of the profits businesses hope to achieve. So it's very important to manage cash flow and spending in order for your business to be successful.

A very common trait among successful business owners is that they work to build increased value in their businesses through reinvestment of their profits into the business for future growth. Then they apply strategies for effective use of resources and careful management of cash flow and debt, so that one day they may be able to sell or cash out of their business. They're seeking financial freedom just like you.

Now, if you imagine your family finances as a business, how would you manage things to accomplish these same objectives? First, you have a job, and possibly your spouse also has a job. Thus, you are both selling a service that is in demand and you are receiving compensation for said services. You are both partners in this business, and your combined salaries represent the business revenues. Your business also has some perks, like insurance protection for health, life, and disability that protect your most valuable resources: you and your ability to work. Next, you will need to invest in some equipment for reliable transportation (cars), communication with your partner (cell phones), and accessibility to information and communication with your home and office (computers). These expenditures are justifiable in that they assist you in selling your services and making and managing your money. You'll need to provide food, clothing, and lodging for your key people so that they continue to be productive. They'll also need some incentives like paid vacations, holiday parties, and time off with family and friends. The bottom line is that you want to provide all these things for your most valued people. As manager of the business, you simply need to make sure that there is sufficient cash flow to pay for these services and still have a good solid profit margin left in the checking account to build the future of your business. With that remaining profit, we can then find a tax-advantaged strategy for investing in the growth of the business and other lifestyle improvements.

As revenues from our services increase, we can buy more goods and services, reward our most valued employees, and continue to reinvest a consistent percentage of revenues back into the business for future growth.

ACTION ITEMS

Treat your family finances like a business and learn how businesses manage money.

Consider taking an accounting or business administration course at a local college.

YOU ARE LIKE A MONEY-MAKING MACHINE

I like to tell people that as they work or run a business, they are like a money-making machine. Essentially, as you work in your profession, you are the mechanism that generates income. Thus, your compensation is the amount of money your machine can print each pay period or each year. Like any other machine, if you don't update its features—such as with continuing education and new ideas—it can lose effectiveness, slow down production, or even become obsolete. You should also allow your machine to have down time (vacation) for maintenance, to be well oiled and keep the gears running smoothly. There's also the possibility that your machine could break down or need repairs along the way. This is why it's important to have disability insurance and an emergency savings fund to make sure money continues to be printed during reparation periods or when you cannot work.

In this day of technological advances that seem to move at the speed of sound, it is not hard to understand the concept of obsolescence. Machines can and will become outdated very quickly. It always amazes me how a smartphone or tablet that just two years ago seemed like the eighth wonder of the world is now ready for the trash bin. So it should be no surprise that eventually your machine will not run, and it is important to plan for buying a new and different machine when that day comes. Is there anyone who would not feel the need to buy a new car if their current vehicle kept breaking down and reached the point of no return? Of course not! Unthinkable!

Imagine now that your business receives revenue from your own money-making machine! Maybe it is in your basement or garage, but that doesn't matter, it simply prints money. That's how your business makes a profit. It's reasonable to assume that you would do everything you can to protect and maintain that machine. It's also reasonable to assume that you would invest in the development of that machine to improve efficiency and possibly produce more money. There is little doubt that you would prepare to upgrade the technology and/ or buy a replacement for that machine should it reach the end of its working life, as all machines eventually do. A wise businessperson would understand that machines depreciate over time and that the business will need to prepare for the purchase of a new machine in order to continue to be profitable and take care of the key people in the company.

THE COST OF PROCRASTINATION IS FAR GREATER THAN THE PRICE OF SACRIFICE

The idea is to think of your new machine as something that can help provide you with complete financial freedom. This is a different kind of machine, with adaptive technology that upgrades itself with very little maintenance. The machine is so advanced that, based on what you put into it, it can distribute a check to you each month for a long period of time, possibly the rest of your life. This income may allow you to do the things you've always wanted to do but were too busy to do while you were keeping the old machine running. You see, this new machine is called a *Personal Retirement Machine (PRM)*, and its technology is unsurpassed. It incorporates a kind of adaptive technology that may never become obsolete. Your current machine is simply a working machine with gears and grease, spare parts, squeaks, aches, and pains. The beauty of financial freedom is that you use the proceeds from your working machine to buy a new, technologically advanced machine that provides you with a check without you needing to go to work. No matter what you do with your time, your Personal Retirement Machine is designed to send you a check every month!

With the proper planning and the discipline to save the money needed to achieve financial freedom, you may acquire your own Personal Retirement Machine. With that machine, your dreams may become a reality, and you could be able to buy the best car you ever imagined or maybe travel by RV and take your grandchildren on a cross-country trip. Having grown up in the Boston area, I've always enjoyed the ocean, so a 40-ft. cabin cruiser motorboat and travels to Nantucket are in my dreams. Or maybe you'd prefer not to travel much but to live on the ocean or spend a lot of time on a golf course or build a really cool photography studio in your home. So if it's boating, country club living, or an RV you seek as part of your financial freedom, you may have it with a well-built Personal Retirement Machine.

While in many cases your working machine is not able to provide you with these things, your Personal Retirement Machine may. Does this type of technology interest you? Given the vast capabilities of this technology and the ultimate value of a consistent cash flow, how much would you be willing to pay for this machine? Is it reasonable to assume that it would be worth a degree of sacrifice and hard work to save the money to buy one? I have yet to meet anyone who wouldn't want a Personal Retirement Machine, just a lot of people who aren't sure how to get one.

Whenever a waiter or vendor asks me, "Can I get you anything else, sir?" or "Is there anything else I can do for you?" I say, "Yes, I'd like a bag of $50's please!"

Well, they said anything!

What if I told you that the federal government is offering you a bag of $50 bills? How about if once every week those $50 bills came in the form of interest-free loans to help purchase your PRM? That's right—good old Uncle Sam is stepping up and offering you an opportunity to borrow money interest-free each year to put toward the purchase of your PRM. How do I get one of those loans, you might ask? Consider investing in your 401(k) plan. Let's assume that you're in a 28 percent marginal federal tax bracket (the tax rate on the last dollar of your earnings), and you contribute $400 per month

($92.31 per week) to your plan as a traditional 401(k) contribution. The fact that you are able to have this contribution deducted from your paycheck before it's taxed means that Uncle Sam is lending you $112 per month (the tax you would otherwise have paid) or $1,344 per year to help your cause. The income tax rules in your home state will vary, however, there may be additional state tax savings as well. So it only costs you $288 per month out of your paycheck to have $400 deposited into your account! Not only that, but Uncle Sam won't tax your interest, dividends, or capital gains (allowing you to use more of his money to reinvest for future growth) until after you build your Personal Retirement Machine and it begins sending you checks.

So let's examine this new machine and how it works. First, the cost for your Personal Retirement Machine will be based mostly on your preretirement income and the percentage of that income you wish to have to achieve financial freedom. You may also wish to add certain features. For example, you may want your monthly output to increase over time to account for inflation, or you may have a special goal such as a vacation home and a lump sum needed to obtain it. The cost of your PRM will be directly related to the amount of money you want it to provide for you over time.

For the purpose of this discussion, let's build a hypothetical machine with features that are consistent with standard rules of thumb for financial freedom. It is commonly accepted by the financial community that most people will need between 65 percent and 80 percent of their regular earnings to live comfortably in retirement and to achieve financial freedom. Therefore, a good rule of thumb is that you would need approximately 70 to 75 percent of your preretirement income to comfortably enjoy financial freedom. This range is provided that you are not encumbered by significant debts at the time you desire to enter this new phase of your financial life. We can anticipate that Social Security will provide you with approximately 20 to 25 percent of your preretirement income. Therefore, you will want your Personal Retirement Machine to provide you with an income of approximately 50 percent of your preretirement income. You may also want to project that the income will increase each year to account for inflation and that your PRM will be able to provide cash distributions for approximately 30 years or longer.

These percentages are all based off of your income in the years immediately before financial freedom and will vary based on your income level, spending goals, and debt levels at that time. I would estimate, for the average person or family making between $75,000 and $100,000 per year (projected preretirement income), the starting price range for their PRM would be from approximately $750,000 to in excess of $1,000,000. However, the higher your income during your working years, the greater the amount of income you will need your PRM to produce. Therefore, for someone making $200,000 or more per year preretirement, the cost could be in the range of $2,000,000 to $3,000,000.

Most often when I tell people the price tag for their PRM they have such sticker shock that their face draws a blank, with their eyes rolling back into their head as if I shot an arrow through their heart. Unfortunately, many of them jump to the conclusion that because the numbers are big they have no realistic chance of getting there. Don't give up before trying! No one has ever been successful at achieving something of value if they believed they couldn't do it.

The first thing I would suggest is to do yourself justice by conducting sufficient financial planning to calculate and determine your number: the amount of income you will need for financial freedom and the expected cost for your PRM. Then develop a clear understanding of what it will take to get there in terms of regular savings amounts in a layaway plan. Even if it seems like having a PRM is out of your reach based on the price tag, you may be surprised to find that it is indeed possible once you break it down to a weekly payroll deduction amount. If this still sounds too expensive, I would say that if you could afford to buy a machine that could potentially keep printing money for you to enjoy for the rest of your life, how much would you be willing to pay for it? Consider the value of having a well-designed mechanism that could provide continuous payments for 20 or 30 years. In addition, how valuable would it be if your PRM could keep printing money for future generations as well? Consider how your children and grandchildren might look back and honor how special the original owner was.

When you consider the potential power of a PRM, you can imagine the possibilities as they fit into your personal vision of your future. Most of us then can understand why something as phenomenal as this would be expensive and/or difficult to obtain. However, if I showed you how you could do it, wouldn't you agree it's worth buying? Interestingly, with reasonably good business management, it doesn't cost too much at all. Remember the family business and how part of your revenue must be reinvested for future growth. We have discussed how businesses also need to put money aside to replace essential business equipment as it becomes obsolete. Well, just like your smartphone will seem slow and dysfunctional in a couple of years, the idea of working under stress every day to make a living will get old and become increasingly difficult. At some point in your future, the physical and mental need to reward yourself and your family with quality of life in terms of lifestyle and freedom will become paramount. The Personal Retirement Machine is the equipment that your family business needs to replace the obsolete equipment. If you practice good business methods and cash management, the cost boils down to two simple things: common sense and sacrifice. You might ask what kind of sacrifice.

Sacrifice is the intelligence to know the value of allocating resources toward the achievement of a future goal, as opposed to expending them for short-term gratification.

ACTION ITEMS

Begin to make a list of your retirement/financial freedom goals such as:

- *What age would you like to begin?*

- *What are your top goals or priorities for travel, hobbies, and major purchases?*

- *Will you be relocating your residence?*

Consider these goals and objectives without regard for what you think you can afford but rather focus on what you want to afford.

Review your debts and consider what debts may remain when you reach your desired age of financial freedom.

Establish a plan to assure debt reduction during your working years.

CHAPTER 3

FINANCIAL FREEDOM PLANNING

THE BASIC TRUTH

I like to tell my clients that the idea of retirement has changed dramatically over time. Most people are more active during their golden years than their parents were during their retirement. They often do new things such as learning a craft, researching matters of interest, teaching, exercising more regularly, and taking part in the things they always wanted to do. In fact, modern day "retirement" by definition isn't really retirement at all. Ideally, retirement should equate to financial freedom—thus the reason I prefer the term "financial freedom." *It means the ability to do the things you enjoy doing, while living the lifestyle you prefer and having the freedom to do that without concern for money.* There may be no better way to experience freedom than to have financial freedom.

The first step in achieving financial freedom is to establish a plan to get there. However, if you're not already participating in a retirement savings strategy, don't put off contributing to your 401(k) or other qualified retirement plan until you get around to having a financial plan prepared. Start contributing right away, and you may then update your contribution amounts once your financial plan is complete.

Financial planning is the culmination of your dreams, your desires, and your vision of the future, combined with your current financial and familial circumstances. The process should include any and all of your special circumstances, needs, and objectives. The first step toward achieving success is to have a well-thought-out financial plan, addressing your goals, objectives, and core needs. Using that plan as a guide for your financial decisions is one of the most effective methods for accomplishing long-term financial goals.

When thinking about the reasons to create and follow a financial plan, please consider this. This is a process that, if ignored, will likely cause you to reach a point in life where you'll feel regret. You will wish that you had been disciplined enough to make the commitment to following a plan sooner in your life. The result may be a financial reality that you'll need to save a substantially higher percentage of your income to make up for the resulting deficiency. Many people simply won't have the wherewithal to do that. The knowledge of what is needed for you to be successful in fulfilling your goals is a fundamental requirement. In order to effectively establish your goals, you must first accurately assess your objectives for later in life. This is why qualified financial planners can be far more valuable than a web-based financial calculator. Their experience in guiding people to meet financial goals can bring to light strategies that the average person often overlooks.

After years of experience providing financial planning for many different people, I can guarantee two things:

- One: personal plans and goals will change over time.

- Two: without a plan, a person's emotions may lead them in the wrong direction—for example, selling stocks at the wrong time.

Just as having a well-thought-out financial plan is critical to achieving success; reviewing that plan periodically is equally important. With a financial plan established, you have a track on which to run and an established guide to indicate if and when you have gone away from your path to success. By reviewing that plan periodically, you can make it adaptive to your changing needs and desires. The one constant is that the retirement planning section only grows in importance as time passes.

The real truth about achieving financial freedom is that it has gotten much harder to achieve your income goals than it was for prior generations. Individuals and families have been faced with less and less support from their employer. People are living longer, and there's increased risk of outliving their money. We have an aging population and a shrinking base of Social Security taxpayers. Our ability to rely on Social Security is also shrinking. The cost of health care is rising significantly faster than the general inflation rate. The cost of living is rising faster than your Social Security benefits as well as the returns on your savings in conservative vehicles such as CDs and money markets.

When my parents were raising a family, retirement planning was a lot easier. To them, it was retirement, which meant slowing down. When our parents or grandparents (depending on whether you're age 55 or age 30) were planning for their retirement, they had much less to be concerned with than we do today. So long as their mortgage and other major debts were paid off, they were often well prepared. For their generation, an approximate average of two-thirds of their income was provided through a combination of Social Security and their employer-sponsored pension plan. Add some personal savings, and they retired with 70 to 75 percent of their preretirement income. Perfect! Unfortunately, most of us do not have such a luxury today.

The number of employers offering pension plan benefits is shrinking each year. The benefits of those remaining pensions are also shrinking or being frozen. Companies simply can't afford these benefits while trying to compete in a global economy. According to the US Department of State, in 1965 there were 170,000 private pension plans in place in the United States. By 1997 that number had dropped to 53,000. In a 2002 report titled "Trends in Defined Benefit Pension Plans," The Pension Benefit & Guarantee Corporation states that the total number of pension plans dropped from 114,000 in 1985 to just 32,500 in 2002. As of 2013, the total number of pension plans in the United States is at an all-time low of 22,697. The report also indicates that the number of active pensions in the United States will continue to decline by 3 to 7 percent per year depending on the size of the plan, with smaller employer plans being terminated at the fastest rate. Watson Wyatt has reported that from 1997 through 2008, nearly 50 percent of the Fortune 100 companies in the United States terminated their pension plans. In 2009, major companies such as Wells Fargo, Cigna, and Anheuser Busch froze their pension plans, leaving only 30 percent of the Fortune 100 companies maintaining pensions. In their 2009 report titled "The Disappearing Defined Benefit Pension…," the Social Security Administration states that "the proportion of private wage and salary workers participating in defined benefit plans" had dropped to 20 percent by 2008. By 2011, that number had dropped to 18 percent. I suspect that number will continue to decline going forward.

So how do we overcome these changes and the challenge to create our own wealth in retirement? *Maximize the benefits of your 401(k).* I believe your 401(k) is one of the most powerful wealth creation tools available today. For most of us, it represents a clear path to success in financial freedom planning. When you consider the benefits (see chapter 8) of tax-deferred growth and the fact that you can have money deducted from your paycheck before it's taxed, it makes saving money much easier. Add to that your ability to have your savings invested into a diverse portfolio of investment alternatives, and you have a very good framework with which to create wealth. If your employer matches your contributions or makes a profit-sharing contribution, that's like getting a tax-favored raise built directly into your personal wealth creation plan. Simply put, a 401(k) provides you with a very powerful vehicle to build wealth over time.

So what is wrong with 401(k) plans? Nothing at all! (While there are some advisors and/or financial writers who state that there are problems with 401(k)s as if you shouldn't use them, I have yet to see those people illustrate a better method for building wealth (particularly when considering the savings habits of the average American). The simple fact is that the biggest problem with 401(k)s is the way in which employees use them or neglect to use them. It's true that some plan sponsors have not designed their plans optimally and that some small employer plans have investments with high fees, but these issues are being addressed by ERISA (see ERISA sect. 408(b)(2)), and the quality of 401(k) plans is improving. These plans will continue to improve through consumer awareness from both employers and their valued employees.

Fees charged on investment assets are a justified concern for any investor. The lower your fees, the more earnings you'll tend to keep and the better your opportunity for growth in your portfolio (presuming all else is equal). The fact is the fees charged on investments inside 401(k) plans may be less on average than fees charged by personal investment brokers. In the 401(k) plans that we manage, our optimal plan design concept is based in part on lower investment expenses vs. those charged for personal investment account management. It's like getting a group discount for your investment portfolio. Therefore, cost is not necessarily a negative—in fact, it could be another positive to attribute to 401(k) investing.

From a benefit standpoint, I agree that it is easier for an employer to reduce your compensation by cutting your profit-sharing or 401(k)-matching benefits than it would be if you had a pension plan. However, you or your friend may be keeping your job as a result of an employer's ability to adjust their overhead through reduced 401(k) contributions, as opposed to cutting jobs. While a particular employer's 401(k) plan may not always provide as much of a retirement benefit as you would like, this is not what is wrong with 401(k) plans; it is more likely what is wrong with the economy and the labor market. In weaker economies, it may be harder to procure retirement benefits from your employer. However, most employers would prefer to reward their employees for the growth and success of their company. Profit sharing and 401(k) plans give them an easy-to-implement, tax-favored way to do so. Keep in mind that financial freedom planning is a long-term journey; the economy and corporate profits will go through cycles both good and bad over that time frame, as will the investment markets. The key to your success is to be in the game through these cycles and continue building your financial future.

The first step in maximizing your 401(k) plan benefits is to determine the right amount to put into your plan. To do this, you must first establish a true understanding of your compensation. The fact is most people don't fully understand their compensation. Therefore, they do not properly allocate funds to their 401(k) plan. Put another way, many employees have it backward! They receive their paycheck, base their standard of living on it, and then try to save something from what little is left after they buy the things they want and need. It's not uncommon to see people exceed their spendable income and create increasing debt loads. This exacerbates their problem, as debt service costs (interest) reduce their future disposable income and thus further reduce their savings capacity. Unfortunately, that scenario just doesn't work out in the long run. To be successful in creating wealth at any level, you must first take an honest look at your compensation for what it is and what it is not.

Even substantial wage earners must carefully examine their cash flow strategy when it comes to wages, savings, taxes, and spending. Keep in mind that your standard of living during your working years greatly influences your standard of living in the realm of financial freedom. Therefore, the amount of savings you'll need to put away today in order to be successful in your later years is a similar percentage of your compensation as that of a more moderate income earner. In short, you'll likely need to save double the amount of money if you earn $150,000 than if you earn $75,000.

ACTION ITEMS

Review your current 401(k) payroll deduction amount. Determine how long it's been since you updated the contribution level and if you are using a percentage of pay as your contribution or a flat dollar amount. If you are using a flat dollar amount as your contribution, calculate the equivalent percentage of pay, and change your contribution to that percentage of pay, rounding up to the nearest whole percentage.

Take this opportunity to review your contribution level in comparison to your employer's matching contributions. If your contributions are not at least enough to receive the maximum employer match, consider increasing your contribution to that level while you're at it!

UNDERSTANDING YOUR COMPENSATION

Your Personal Retirement Machine cannot be purchased by borrowing money or taking out a mortgage on your house. You can only buy it by making payments in advance, just like putting something on layaway. However, as previously mentioned, Uncle Sam will provide you with an interest-free loan as a percentage of the amount you deposit into your layaway accounts if you desire. If your family finances are like a family business, in order to keep that business viable you need to update the machinery to keep cash flowing in. Therefore, it is necessary that some of the money that your family business creates must be put into the layaway plan in order to be able to buy the new Personal Retirement Machine to provide you with financial freedom when your working machine breaks down. In other words, no matter how much your family business earns, part of your income today must be dedicated to the future of the business. This fundamental fact of financial life is too often ignored or simply escapes the minds of many people. As a result, those people aren't able to buy a Personal Retirement Machine that does what they need when they really need to have it.

To truly understand the effective use of the family business dollars to promote growth and success over time, you must first understand your compensation and how to allocate those dollars to fund the needs of both the business and the people working in it (you and your family). The first thing you must know is that not all of your compensation is spendable compensation. Your compensation should be broken down into two primary categories: *savings compensation* and *spending compensation*. Savings compensation can be allocated according to your goals for buying a home, your children's education, and, most importantly, your financial freedom. Spending compensation can then be further broken down into two categories: essential spending and discretionary spending. *Essential spending* is what you pay for the necessities in life, such as food, shelter, clothing, and health care. *Discretionary spending* is for things like entertainment, dining out, recreational toys, and vacationing.

Successful businesses often invest time and money in conducting research, hiring consultants, and creating business plans based on this research and advice. This enables businesspeople to operate in an efficient and productive way with a clear vision of their objectives and just how to manage their day-to-day activities to accomplish them. People who are successful financially do something quite similar. They have a financial plan prepared in which they've invested time and money for research and advice. They understand their compensation and, with the help of their advisor, have an efficient way of allocating their compensation to meet their current and future needs.

Let's put this concept into action and consider how a family business would view cash flow. We have revenue (salaries minus taxes), and from that we pay our fixed expenses, such as mortgage/rent, food, utilities, and other necessities. Once we pay our fixed expenses, we are left with gross profit or what is technically called gross margin. From this marginal income, we must allocate funds for reinvestment in the future of our family business, and what remains is discretionary income. Discretionary income is your favorite kind of income because it's the money we can do whatever we want with. This is what we have left after our fundamental necessities are paid for and plans for our future are put in place. Now we have the flexibility to enjoy the funds we have, knowing that our commitments have been met. This is the positive income you can spend on entertainment, vacations, and buying things for your comfort and pleasure.

However, the key to a successful business is to know the danger of spending in excess of that discretionary income, as this may have adverse consequences down the road, such as excess debts, interest expenses, and insufficient savings.

The reinvestment of profits back into the business is a critical element in creating the opportunity for future success for the people in the business. It is the foundation upon which the family business will have the ability to grow and protect itself from unforeseen events. It's also what allows the business to open new opportunities or invest in things like a new building (vacation home) or another business. Imagine a technology company that doesn't reinvest some of its gross profits into the research and development of new technologies. It won't be long before their company's technology becomes obsolete and they fall behind the competition. There have been many companies that have met that fate and, as a result, gone out of business. Consider a medical device company that fails to invest in researching new and improved ways to treat patients. Surely you can imagine how that business may shrink over time as other innovative people discover new and improved treatments. Similarly, reinvesting in your family business is the key to building that business and fostering the growth and development of discretionary income.

It has been aptly stated by many a businessperson that if your business isn't growing, it's dying. A business simply cannot stand pat or stay the same. It must evolve and grow. I am a confirmed believer in this concept. Growing your discretionary income through careful cash flow management and regular savings is the key to growing the family business. If you don't invest in your future, the day will come when you no longer have sufficient discretionary income. By then, it may be too late to turn back, and you may never have discretionary income again! That's a bad day.

To avoid this fate, it's important to recognize that a percentage of your earnings, *likely between 10 and 15 percent of your gross pay,* must be set aside before you can determine how much you have to spend on discretionary items. Thus, a person who earns gross compensation of $50,000 has to put a minimum of $5,000 away for future needs and recognize only the remaining $45,000 as gross income. From that 90 percent number, after taxes and fixed expenses are paid, you can determine how much you have to spend on discretionary items. Fortunately, there are ways of reducing the percentage of your income that must be considered savings compensation. This is the subject of further discussion.

You may also wish to formulate a monthly/annual budget to keep track of your spending habits. I advise my clients not to be threatened by a budget, as I don't suggest using it as a way of restricting your financial freedom. A budget is a great way to look back over the month or year and see where your money went. This can be a useful tool in cash flow management going forward. Your financial plan can provide you with a more specific percentage of your total compensation, which should be considered savings compensation, that you will need to put on layaway to buy your Personal Retirement Machine.

ACTION ITEMS

Establish a financial plan through a qualified financial advisor, and follow the plan.

Determine the proper percentage of your total income that is savings compensation. Consistently reinvest that amount in your family business to grow your wealth.

Take advantage of the interest-free loan that Uncle Sam is offering you in your 401(k).

Put your Personal Retirement Machine on a layaway plan as soon as possible.

CHAPTER 4

CREATING YOUR LONG-TERM FINANCIAL PLAN

UNDERSTANDING THE IMPORTANCE OF FREE CASH FLOW

The most common response I hear from people who complain that they can't afford to treat some of their income as saving compensation is that they claim they have no money left after they pay their bills. If this was your reaction, you're not alone. However, there is an answer to your problem, and it lies in your ability to create *free cash flow*, and the good news is anyone can do it.

You've most likely heard the phrase "cash is king." Well, without cash flow there can be no cash. Without free cash flow, ultimately there will be no cash. So what is free cash flow, and how do we get it? One of the first things you'll need to do to create free cash flow is to understand the impact of spending and debt on cash flow. Next you'll need to understand what portion of your household income is savings compensation versus spending compensation so that you have a clear goal for the amount of free cash flow you want to create.

The difference between cash flow and free cash flow is that cash flow is simply the money flowing into and out of your hands. Essentially, it is defined as the total amount of funds that flow through your pockets in a given period. *Free cash flow is the money that flows into your pockets but doesn't flow out in a given period. It is from free cash flow that wealth is created. By clearing the way for free cash flow through debt reduction and smart spending habits, you may then invest that free cash into the building blocks of your financial future.*

The process of creating free cash flow starts by identifying behaviors that cause a lack of free cash. In some cases, people who seem to have ample financial resources can make mistakes in establishing spending habits—mistakes that take away cash flow and result in a deterioration of their financial well-being. The following is a real-life case study that speaks to the effect of poor cash flow management. The names and locations used are fictitious and in no way represent a particular individual.

Ken is a husband, father of two healthy kids, and a senior programming specialist for a software company. He lives in a sleepy bedroom community outside of Fort Lee, New Jersey, just outside of New York City. Before we met Ken, the company he worked for was purchased by a publicly traded international software company. In addition to Ken's wages, he had received stock options for almost ten years prior. When the company was sold, his stock options were worth $2 million after taxes.

Another client who worked for the same company referred Ken to us. Based on the data collected, we created his plan.

Before the windfall, Ken and his wife, Margaret, were doing quite well. Ken earned $100,000 in net income and saved almost $25,000 per year. They had saved about $250,000 in their IRAs, excluding his stock options. They owed about $385,000 between their car loans, mortgage, and a second mortgage—debt that had grown over time.

Given that Ken and Margaret had significant debt, using part of the proceeds from the sale of his stock to become debt-free may have been advisable. The reduction of all that debt could have cleared enough free cash flow that they could potentially live off their portfolio instead of continuing to earn wages. Ken had missed much of their kids' lives as a high-tech executive, and now he would finally have a chance to enjoy his family. Ken had other plans for the use of his capital.

He let us manage his $250,000 IRA and began building a dream house for his family in Tarrytown, New York. He planned to increase the "investment" in their home from $600,000 to $2.4 million. He felt all his hard work had finally paid off. He could at last give his family the better things in life. The dream house quickly became a nightmare, as it took longer and cost more than anticipated, with almost $450,000 in cost overruns.

At the very least, Ken could have kept his mortgage balance low on the new home. But after talking to his mortgage broker, he decided to borrow 90 percent of the home's value with "cheap money," and then he used the remaining cash to put down payments on several investment real estate properties to parlay his small fortune into a large one.

Ken and his wife soon upgraded their furniture, cars, private schools, and just about everything else. Without any wage increases, Ken's personal expenses went from just $75,000 per year pre-windfall to $225,000 annually post-windfall.

In no time, Ken owned several "cannot lose" investment properties, with all their associated mortgages, property taxes, insurances, and repairs. His real estate broker assured him he would make money on the appreciation of his investment property. Ken's future wealth hummed and glowed in his mind. Margaret didn't understand high finance, but she had a bad feeling about it all. The property's carrying costs added another $225,000 per year on top of his $225,000 in personal expenses.*

Now, with only $100,000 coming in and $450,000 going out, the cash was going down very quickly, in spite of a vast net worth.

Have you ever wondered how rock stars or lottery winners or trust fund babies can lose it all, even though they have enough wealth to buy a small country? The answer lies in cash flow. Or, better stated, the answer lies in the lack of cash flow.

THE IDEAL CASH FLOW ... FREE CASH FLOW

What is free cash flow? It is the amount of money you have after paying all your bills and purchases. If you spend more than you make, there are symptoms: you have no cash and have a high level of financial stress, increasing debt, and a lot of interest payments. You are in a negative cash flow position, meaning that more money

*Keep in mind that investing involves risk, including the risk of loss. Investment decisions should be based on an individual's own goals, time horizon, and tolerance for risk.

is going out than coming in. Other symptoms that may accompany a negative cash flow state are stress within your family, disappointment, and frustration.

If you spend less than you make, there are more pleasant symptoms. You have savings, you are reducing debt or have very little of it, and you have a positive financial outlook. This is a positive cash flow state—more money is coming in than going out. Some other symptoms that accompany a positive cash flow state are excitement about achieving your goals, planning vacations, and appreciation for your hard work.

Without good free cash flow, the chances of reaching your savings compensation goals are slim to none. If you don't achieve your savings goals, then you will not likely enjoy the benefits of a properly designed Personal Retirement Machine. That is why we put so much emphasis on this topic. Improving your free cash flow should be your number-one priority. It truly is that important to ensuring your financial freedom.

Like Ken and Margaret, the lesson of cash flow is usually learned from pain rather than discipline. Some people learn its importance from job loss, cash-draining investment choices, health problems, economic downturns, or needy adult kids. Many people, unfortunately, never learn its importance and continue to struggle financially.

As you read this chapter today, where are you in terms of cash flow?

- Do you have *great* cash flow? We define *great* cash flow as saving 50 percent or more of every dollar you make in net income.

- Do you have *good* cash flow? We define *good* cash flow as saving 10 to 49 percent of net income.

- Do you have *poor* cash flow? We define *poor* cash flow as saving less than 10 percent of your net income.

If you're not happy with your cash flow, you can do something about it. Yes, it takes discipline and can involve some difficult choices, but in the long term, getting a firm handle on cash flow is the best thing you can do for yourself and your family.

GREAT CASH FLOW—WHAT TO DO

If you are saving 50 percent or more of your net income—well done! Consider yourself amongst a small minority. You could stop here and skip on to the next chapter. However, with great cash flow already, I'm guessing you're driven to read on to improve things even more.

One small suggestion: Use that great cash flow to retire any remaining debt. Most likely you've already done so, but if not, this step will help you save even more down the road. Keep up the good work!

GOOD CASH FLOW—WHAT TO DO

If you are saving 10 to 49 percent of your net income, you may be well on your way to becoming wealthy. To make your position even better, use at least half of your monthly savings to clear up debts. This may seem obvious, but the following illustration will help drive home this point.

SUZY, THE "GOOD CASH FLOW" EXAMPLE

Suzy, a 50-something flight attendant from Miami, is doing very well in spite of going through a difficult *divorce. She earns $80,000 per year from a combination of wages and alimony.*

As a flight attendant, Suzy has learned the importance of having a backup plan since she has already been through many financial struggles, countless industry layoffs, pay cuts, and corporate restructuring, as well as a divorce from a pilot who had too much fun on his international layovers. She has been preparing for a rainy day for a long time. In fact, she saves 20 percent of every paycheck.

"I can only count on myself," says Suzy, "So my financial future is in my own hands."

When we looked at Suzy's spending, her largest expense by far (like most Americans) was her debt payments. She owed $197,500 between her car, credit card, and condo mortgage. Her total payments were $2,360 per month, or $28,320 per year, roughly half of her monthly expenses.

Without this debt burden, her other monthly and annual expenses would have been $3,000 per month or $36,000 per year.

According to her plan, Suzy will pay $20,000 extra per year toward her debt, on top of her car, credit card, and mortgage payments of $28,320. As a result, by paying a total of $48,320 per year, she will be debt-free in four and a half years and earning enough from her investments to cover her current expenses in six years.

As you can see, by using at least half of your free cash flow, you can begin to pay off your debt in a very short time. Use Suzy as an example. Write in your journal what you can do to pay off your consumer debt in no more than four years and no more than ten years for your mortgages. Paying off your debt could significantly increase your cash flow over the long term.

POOR CASH FLOW—WHAT TO DO

Are you saving less than 10 percent of your net income? Are you just keeping your head above water? Are you a slave to your lifestyle, increasing your debt or just consuming your net pay every year?

How do you get the cash flow engine started? From the above example, it is easy to see the impact of getting out of debt. But if you are just barely paying the bills, you need to add one more step. You need to spend less on each of your five largest bills and increase your income.

So how do you do it? Make a date with your significant other to address the situation. Get a babysitter for the kids and a bottle of wine, and set aside the necessary time to truly look at where your extra spending is coming from. If you are divorced or single, sit down with a trusted advisor.

Are you eating out too often? Do you live in a home that is more than you can afford? Do you have expensive tastes in cars, clothes, or travel? Figure out what you need to change right now so that you can save an ideal 20 percent.

ACTION ITEM

Write in your financial plan which cash flow condition best describes your situation: great, good, or poor. Follow the appropriate program in the following pages.

Why 20 percent? That way you do not have to spend your whole life stressed out and working. Also, it will make 10 percent in actual savings much more likely because unexpected purchases, repairs, and so on can waylay the best of plans.

Let's look at ways to increase your income and review the top expenses and some possible solutions for cutting costs.

INCREASE YOUR INCOME

What ways can you add more value to your employer to deserve more compensation? Here are some ways to increase your family's income by adding more value:

- Have your spouse work.

- Take on a part-time job.

- Ask for a raise.

- Set up a performance bonus.

- Increase your output.

- Move to a more prosperous area.

- Do something else that pays more.

- Get training, licensing, or a degree.

- Go into sales or into a professional field where the pay is higher.

- Be mentored by successful people who earn more than you while working in the same field as you.

REDUCE EXPENSES AND DEBT

Of all the expenses, debt reduction is the major key to improving cash flow for most families. Here are some ways to reduce debt expenses:

- Set up a plan to pay all non-mortgage debt in four years or less.

- Negotiate lower interest rates, and lock in low fixed rates (avoid adjustable rates).

- Sell assets to pay off debt.

- Consider using retirement assets to pay off debt.

- Stop buying unnecessary "stuff" until debt-free.

- Cut up your credit cards and use cash exclusively.

- Minimize business expenses until debts are paid off.

- Sell toys and unwanted stuff to pay off debt.

- Develop your own creative ways to pay off debt.

REDUCE CHILD-RELATED EXPENSES

By teaching your children how to save, you will not only reduce your expenses now, you will also help make them feel self-sufficient and reduce your expenses in the future. Here are a few pointers:

- Pay for your children's needs, but have your children pay for their own wants.

- Don't create a "welfare state" within the family by supporting or enabling a lifestyle your children cannot support.

- Don't give children or teens credit cards.

- Teach children to limit spending to half of their income, while saving half.

- Encourage kids to also save for college.

- Give kids chores so that they learn to be responsible.

- Consider having kids take subsidized college classes while in high school to reduce college tuition expenses.

- Put teens "in charge" of their expenses, like insurance.

REDUCE VACATION EXPENSES

Travel can be an expensive item for a family. Here are ways to keep costs down:

- Go on company-paid trips.

- Go on tax-deductible trips with your church to help others where sponsorship is available.

- Shop for travel bargains online.

- Set a budget, and limit travel expenses to a targeted amount.
- Visit countries with favorable exchange rates.
- Use frequent flyer miles.

REDUCE INSURANCE EXPENSES

Insurance can be a very high expense. Here are some ways to cut costs:

- Stay healthy: work out, eat right, don't smoke, and get enough rest.
- Bid out life, health, disability, auto, long-term care, and liability insurance regularly.
- Increase your deductibles to lower the policy cost as savings increase.
- If self-employed, have business pay for insurance
- Maintain a good driving record.
- Make fewer claims against your home and auto policies.

REDUCE HOME EXPENSES

One of the largest expense items is your home. Look at ways to reduce these expenses:

- Use cash flow to pay off mortgage sooner.
- Convert variable-rate loans to fixed-rate loans.
- Rent instead of owning a home if you plan on moving within five years.

- Move to a smaller home.

- Bid out insurance costs regularly.

- Get your lender's permission to cancel mortgage insurance once the loan is below 80 percent market value.

- Do not borrow more than 80 percent of your home's value.

- Put off remodeling your home.

- Pay down mortgage with investments.

ACTION ITEM

Make a list of toys you don't need any more and what you plan to do with them now.

REDUCE THE COST OF "TOYS" AND SECOND HOMES

It is amazing what we spend on grown-up toys—boats, motorcycles, airplanes, RVs, and so on. Here are a few ways to make these cost less:

- Sell your toy.

- Buy a less expensive toy.

- Buy fractional interest in a toy.

- Buy with a partner.

- Put a toy into a business.

- Have friends with toys.

- Add up the total cost, calculate the cost per use, and determine whether to own or to rent.

- Use craigslist to get toys cheap.

REDUCE AUTO EXPENSES

Automobiles can represent status as well as mere transportation. Consider these suggestions to reduce your vehicle expenses:

- Keep your cars longer (five years minimum).

- Consider less expensive vehicles with strong records for dependability. Frills are expensive and depreciate in value quickly.

- Consider an extended warranty to minimize car maintenance costs.

- Bid out insurance costs regularly.

- Rent cars for high-mileage trips if you lease your vehicle.

- Sell cars that aren't being used.

- Donate old cars to charity for the tax write-off.

- Get a car with better gas mileage.

- Move closer to work.

- Check the best prices online to help negotiate better pricing at the dealership.

ACTION ITEM

Look at your expenses for the past 12 months, and identify areas of excessive unplanned spending.

REDUCE UNPLANNED EXPENSES

Unplanned expenses can be a major source of expenses. Here are some ways to minimize the costs:

- Carry fewer credit cards with lower limits, and pay them off monthly.

- Limit access by paying a weekly cash allowance to each spouse.

- Never buy groceries if hungry.

- Set a maximum limit you can spend without spousal approval.

- Limit going where you spend—malls, QVC, eBay, Amazon, shopping vacations, or shoe stores.

- Put the most responsible and frugal spouse in charge of the checkbook, and limit money access of the free-spending spouse.

REDUCE REMODELING EXPENSES

Remodeling can send a savings plan out the window. Here are some tips:

- Put off remodeling.
- Check referrals of contractors before hiring.
- Get multiple fixed bids for your remodeling projects.
- Limit remodeling to projects that increase the resale value, like upgrading the bath, kitchen, or curb appeal.
- Do not pay the full balance of a bill until work is completed to your satisfaction.
- Hire an inspector to ensure that work is done before paying the final bill.
- Buy materials from discount stores—Sam's Club, Costco, Amazon, eBay, DirectBuy, craigslist, etc.

REDUCE BUSINESS EXPENSES

If you own a small business, you may be comfortable with expenditures for the business that you wouldn't want to spend money for personally. Consider the following ways to reduce the business expenses:

- Save the first 20 percent of profit, then limit bills to the remaining 80 percent.
- Clamp down on any unnecessary expenses.
- Put systems in place to speed up cash payments into the business and make it hard to approve expenses.
- Buy instead of leasing to avoid future payments.

- Set a price ceiling for hotels, meals, and so on.

- Use windfalls to pay off debt.

- Provide employee incentives for cost-reduction ideas that your company implements.

- If the business has poor income potential, sell it where possible, or shut it down and move on.

- Buy used equipment instead of new.

- Bid out insurance, materials, and professional services regularly.

- Look at each product line, and make sure it adds to the bottom line. Remove unprofitable lines.

- Replace marginal employees quickly.

Now, go through the various expense lists, and pick at least three things you will do to reduce your spending to save a minimum of 20 percent. Yes, 20 percent, because from experience, it takes more than a 10 percent identified reduction to get the results of a 10 percent actual spending reduction.

Remember what we said at the beginning of the chapter—poor cash flow is why many people never achieve their financial goals. Do not put this difficult step off, or you will be in the same boat next year.

WHY MOST PEOPLE NEVER BECOME WEALTHY

Remember Ken and Margaret from the beginning of this chapter? They eventually sold their home and other properties that did not add to their cash flow, even if it meant selling them at a loss. Unfortunately, a decline in the real estate markets came at the worst time. It took about 12 months, but they sold enough property—including their dream home—to reduce their personal and business annual expenses from $450,000 per year to $100,000.

They lost 75 percent of their windfall in two years. They learned an expensive lesson, but now they have a much better understanding of the importance of cash flow.

After their dream house sold, they moved back to their old neighborhood in Fort Lee, New Jersey, in a slightly larger home. They still owe about $115,000 on their new home and have $100,000 in nonretirement funds after paying off their cars. They have their retirement fund that is worth $350,000. In two years, they plan on being debt-free.

This chapter will either be very easy or very hard for you. The payback for doing these exercises is life changing. Once you have done them long enough to build savings, you will be very grateful that you took on the challenge. Decide now that you will do what it takes to free up at least 10 percent of your net pay, and use it to start eliminating your debt.

Use the ideas outlined in this chapter, or make up your own, to eliminate your debt through expense savings. Six months from now you can expect to begin to feel the freedom that a little cash flow can bring.

We have now covered the single most important factor to financial success: creating free cash flow. Now we are ready to address how to increase your investments through the use of free cash flow. But first, let's review:

1. Free cash flow is the single most important factor as to whether you become financially free or become a slave to your lifestyle.

2. To change your cash flow, you must first analyze your income, taxes, and spending.

ACTION ITEMS

Find out how much you currently save as a percentage of your net income.

Your savings is great if you are saving at least 40 percent of every dollar of net income. Keep up the good work!

Your savings is good if you are saving 10 to 40 percent of every net income dollar. Use your free cash flow to retire your debt in no more than four years. Every year, you should retire 25 percent of your consumer debt and stop adding to the debt pile. Once your consumer debt is gone, use everything you were using to pay off debt to increase investments into your 401(k) and other investments with earnings potential. Use half of your free cash flow to pay down and retire your mortgage. Before you know it, you'll have eliminated the average American family's largest expense: debt.

Your savings is poor if you are saving less than 10 percent of your net income. You need to reduce your largest bills until you have a planned free cash flow of 20 percent. Then, follow the plan of good savers for even less financial stress.

If getting started on reducing debt is overwhelming to you at this point in your life, be sure to connect with a trusted financial advisor who can guide you through the process. Do not let yourself be overwhelmed. Take control of the situation. You will be glad you did.

N.B. This example is hypothetical and does not represent any specific securities product and/or insurance policy. Actual results will vary. This is for information purposes only. You should consult with your attorney and accountant for legal and tax advice.

CHAPTER 5

SEVEN RULES FOR SUCCESSFUL RETIREMENT INVESTING

THE POWER OF COMPOUNDING

E arlier in the book, I mentioned that *"the earliest dollars saved are the most valuable retirement income producers."* There's little question about that. Often when I share the staggering numbers of how much it takes to create your own Personal Retirement Machine, people get turned off, thinking that it's out of reach or that it simply isn't worth trying. First and foremost, *the worst thing you can ever do is defeat yourself without trying.* I see this as a universal truth. More to the point, there is incredible potential resulting from the combination of invested money and time. One of the greatest assets an investor can have in his or her portfolio is time. In working toward your wealth accumulation objectives, the more time that passes with money invested, the greater the likelihood you will achieve exceptional returns. In this chapter we review proven techniques for building wealth over time and some simple truths about investing that seem to elude investors over and over again.

I wish to share a true life story that hopefully will help you realize that what seems insurmountable today can be achieved piece by piece over time with relative ease—so long as you apply the fundamental principles of long-term investing. While this information is based on a true story, the information about the person involved, her name, and her employer have been changed to protect her privacy. The investment results described in the story are not an indication of future performance and are not intended as investment advice. *Past performance is not a guarantee of future performance.*

I have a close friend who has the good fortune of having a very successful relative, his Aunt Gladys. Gladys has been quite generous and considerate to him and his cousins throughout their lives. Gladys was a pioneering woman in the business realm and a very successful executive at a major insurance company. She received her secondary education from a prestigious Boston-area university; she majored in statistics, and her goal was to become a teacher. She graduated number two in her class in 1941. She went on to work at an insurance company in Boston and amassed an illustrious record of success and achievement in her career as an executive of the company. Aunt Gladys became the very first female vice president in the history of the company. Fortunately, her employer was proactive in their efforts to promote equal opportunities for women, in large part due to Gladys's efforts in that area and the respect she garnered among her peers. She rose to the position of senior vice president by the mid 1970s. In 1977, she was noted as one of the top 100 women in business in the United States. Shortly thereafter, she was elected president and chief executive officer of a start-up property insurance division within the company. She managed that company to become a $1 billion organization by 1985 when she retired. Gladys is now 94 years old and one of the most amazing people I know.

After establishing her professional career, she was approached by a college in Boston and was asked to join a steering committee made up of some of the most successful women in business. At the time, this well-respected college was an all-female school, and the objective of the steering committee was to develop a curriculum designed to prepare women for success in executive positions and to promote women's rights to equal opportunities in the workplace. Not only did Gladys set an example for the acceptance of women as equals in the workplace, but she went on to establish programs specifically designed to promote women in the workplace at her insurance company. Her company established a department called "Women's Development." This department was dedicated to the proactive advancement of women into executive positions and to building systems to enable women to remain in their chosen career even in motherhood. Aunt Gladys was so deeply committed to the program that the department head for Women's Development became her lifelong friend and companion until she passed away many years later. To this day, this major insurer maintains one of the top day care centers in the area, in-house, for children of their employees.

As a dedicated career woman, Aunt Gladys did not have children of her own. In her extended family, she has eight nieces and nephews, including my close friend, and she has always considered them to be her children. They were all fortunate to have such a close family, and she feels quite fortunate for the love and respect she receives from all of them.

Given Aunt Gladys's success, she felt compelled to share her wealth with her nieces and nephews while they were all "young enough to put it to good use" and so that she would be sure to avoid estate taxes down the road. Each year she gave a gift of approximately $5,000 to each of them as well as her three siblings. That is 11 people!

Aunt Gladys wanted to gift money to her family in part because she saw how they used it to help buy their first home or do special things for their young children, such as sending them to summer camp or taking family vacations. She had the benefit of seeing firsthand how she was improving the quality of her family's lives and how they truly love and appreciate her thoughtfulness. Her gifting program was something that gave her great joy. She took pride in seeing her family's lifestyles enhanced through her generosity.

Some years after she retired, she was unable to continue these generous annual gifts, as her income now relied largely on her investments and the income or growth they provided. Shortly thereafter, in the fall of 1999, Gladys came to me and said that she would like to continue her gifting program for the upcoming Christmas. She thought that she could take money from a mutual fund investment that she had built up substantial assets in and didn't need. However, she was reluctant to do so because she was afraid of the capital gains taxes she'd have to pay in order to liquidate her shares, and she was curious if I had any ideas. First, I asked her how much was involved, and she replied $100,000. Then I asked how much she had invested in the fund. She went on to say that back in 1968 she started to save money in a mutual fund and that over the next year she invested a total of $2,000. I then asked how much more she invested over the years since then, and she said that she stopped after that because her employer began offering a 401(k) plan.

Somewhat stunned, I confirmed, "So Gladys, you invested just $2,000 between 1968 and 1969, and now the fund is worth $100,000. Is that correct?" Yes, she replied. Quite impressed, I immediately began to calculate what that equated to in average annualized returns. To achieve this, she earned an average annual return of approximately 13.45 percent. I suspect that the majority of that came to her in the 1990s during one of the greatest bull markets in stock market history. However, I don't think it's unreasonable to presume that other long-term investors could experience another great bull market over a 20- to 30-year period.

After careful thought, given Aunt Gladys's desire to gift the money to her family yet avoid taxation, I advised her that she could gift shares of the mutual fund in lieu of cash and let each of the recipients choose what to do with their shares. They could choose to hold the shares and hope for continued growth, or they could choose to sell some or all of the shares and use the cash for their personal needs and interests. Should they sell them, they would personally be responsible for the capital gains tax upon liquidation. Needless to say, Gladys thought this was a great idea, and she proceeded to gift the shares to all of them.

Let's examine this set of facts a little closer and determine how $100,000 of wealth was created out of a $2,000 investment. First, a total of $2,000 was invested over a period of approximately 12 months from 1968 through 1969 in a large cap stock mutual fund. This fund was designed to approximate the returns of the S&P 500 Index, an index of 500 of the greatest companies in the United States that is widely considered to be representative of the stock market overall. This $2,000 investment grew to nearly $100,000 in just over 30 years! How did she accomplish this? It's very simple: she deposited $2,000 into a stock mutual fund, reinvested the dividends, and never touched it again for 30 years. This strategy resulted in an investment with a value of approximately $100,000. Sure, she looked at the statements every quarter and saw dividends or capital gains as well as the ups and downs of the share price, but she never touched it! Would you like to review this process one more time? Once she invested the money, there was no further buying or selling, she did not try her hand at market timing, and she did not make any changes based on research reports or magazine articles. Nothing but deposits totaling $2,000 over a 12-month period 30-plus years earlier, resulting in an asset worth nearly $100,000! Would you be interested in this strategy? Try it in your 401(k)!

It wasn't just a simple investment strategy that made Aunt Gladys so successful. She also had patience, fortitude, and a certain discipline to leave her investment alone long enough to reach its full potential. We can't promise that you will have the same results, but what we can say is that these virtues of patience, consistency, and discipline are prerequisites for the potential of long-term investment success.

In order to validate this story, I've researched the historical results of the S&P 500 Index beginning on January 1, 1970 and ending on December 31, 1999 (30 years). I've backed into these numbers such that I've determined how much of an investment would have been required at the beginning of this period to grow to $100,000 by the end of the 30 years. The number of $2,186 does not necessarily represent Aunt Gladys' account balance as of 1/1/1970.

The hypothetical table below looks at the total returns of the S&P 500 Index decade by decade for a similar period as noted above.

While this table does use actual historical returns of the S&P 500 Index, this is not a representation of Aunt Gladys's actual performance, and I cannot promise this will be your result in the future. It is intended to show a pattern, possibly similar to Gladys's strategy, of how a long-term investment can grow over time based on historical stock market returns. With this success story in mind, we can also examine the reasons why taking withdrawals from your 401(k) can be particularly damaging to your financial freedom plan.

Decade	Beginning Value	Avg. Annual Return*	Compound Total Return	Ending Value
1990s	$18,945	18.1%	427.8%	$100,000
1980s	$3,841	17.3%	393.1%	$18,945
1970s	$2,186	5.8%	75.7%	$3,841

Source: www.simplestockinvesting.com
*Includes reinvestment of dividends

What this table shows is that if you had $2,186 invested in the S&P 500 Index on January 1, 1970 and you reinvested all the dividends each year, that investment would have grown to $100,000 by December 31, 1999, approximately 30 years later. (This performance is based on the performance of an index as published by "S&P Dow Jones Indices" and is not intended as an investment recommendation. Past performance is not an indication or a guarantee of future performance.) This assumes of course that at no point did you ever change the investment allocation, take loans from the account, or make any kind of withdrawals from the investment. You can see how the effect of compounding returns profoundly impacts your ability to accumulate wealth. You may also realize that history has shown how one good decade in the market (as represented by the S&P 500 Index) can offer profound growth opportunities. You can also see that time in the market, not market timing, can lead you to riches through your participation in great economic expansions and equity bull markets. There may be points along the way that a professional advisor can offer beneficial portfolio changes; however, you must be careful not to overreact to changes in market conditions. What this table doesn't show you is how much money you may have had if you invested another $2,186 in 1971. The answer is approximately $194,167. Now you can imagine that some level of wealth could have been created if you contributed $2,186 every year for 30 years!

Looking at the table above, you can see that there was very considerable growth in the later years that contributed to the overall average annual return in excess of 13 percent. The success of this investment was greatly influenced by the timing of the great bull market of the 1990s. Bull markets like that come along only once in a great while. However, a 30-year period is a "great while" by investment standards. The key to finding growth opportunities is to remain disciplined and follow the Seven Rules for Successful Retirement Investing, which is discussed in the next section. The cost of violating these fundamental rules of successful investing can be so significant that it has a lasting negative effect on your lifestyle during your later years.

One of the most important of the seven rules is that when it comes to retirement plan investing, you should never take early withdrawals. With that in mind, let's also explore what the damage to Aunt Gladys's ending balance would have been if she made a withdrawal.

If you recall, Aunt Gladys stopped contributing to the mutual fund after putting only $2,000 in it because her employer started a 401(k) plan and she was committed to investing through that program. What if years later she received a statement that showed she had $18,945 in the account and thought that since she was contributing to her employer's 401(k) regularly, this was free money that she could splurge with?

The bottom line is that if she had taken out those funds to use for an extravagant vacation or something else, she would have unwittingly lost more than $81,000 in growth over the next ten years based on the table above and the historic performance of the S&P 500 Index.

While we cannot foresee or guarantee that future performance in the stock market will assimilate past performance, I believe it's reasonable to say that early withdrawals diminish your opportunity to accumulate investment earnings. Those potential earnings could be the difference between a comfortable period of financial bliss in your older years and a struggle to make ends meet for the rest of your life. As this story shows, it's much harder to create that $100,000 of wealth at age 65 than it was when you were 35.

ACTION ITEMS

Write this down in your financial plan. If you don't have a plan, start a plan with these two rules written on the first page.

1) Never take withdrawals from your 401(k) plan.

2) Never violate Rule #1.

Review your current 401(k) contribution level. Conduct a simple budget analysis to determine if you have the ability to increase your contributions.

Determine if you have a loan outstanding on your 401(k), and develop a plan to pay it off as quickly as possible. Be sure your plan to pay off the 401(k) loan does not inhibit or reduce your ability to effectively manage other debts and debt service costs.

SEVEN RULES FOR SUCCESSFUL RETIREMENT INVESTING

I recognize that many of my readers don't have 30 years before they begin to draw on their savings. However, no matter how much time you have until you achieve financial freedom, don't forget that you may live 20 to 30 years after that point or longer. So it is not unreasonable to presume that investments made today may still have the potential to create great wealth in your future. It's never too late to begin. When it comes to planning for financial independence over shorter periods, it becomes more important to have a commitment to a plan of action and an established mathematical process to determine your appropriate savings amount. Of course, this may mean larger contributions if you haven't built a substantial nest egg. If that's your situation, a higher percentage of your income may need to be considered savings compensation.

There is also a factor of good fortune or timing involved. The shorter your investment time horizon, the more harmful a bear market will be to your overall success and the more careful you'll need to be in establishing your investment allocation strategy. Obviously, we all want and need to experience the high-growth trends in the investment markets. Although it cannot be guaranteed, over the course of long-term investment horizons, chances are you'll experience more years of positive returns than negative in the stock market. However, investments over a shorter term period rely more on the current state of the economy and world events. Fortunately, there are financial planning strategies that can be employed to minimize the effect of negative market trends while enabling you to continue to invest for growth. We will continue to explore these methods as we proceed.

Regardless of your age or the amount of money that you have, the 401(k) plan and other qualified retirement plans offer investors some of the most advantageous features for favorable investing. If you follow these Seven Rules for Successful Retirement Investing, this may give you your best opportunity to achieve your goals.

RULE #1:
TAKE ADVANTAGE OF UNCLE SAM'S INTEREST-FREE LOANS.

The most obvious and beneficial 401(k) tool is the tax benefit of investing pretax through payroll deduction. In other words, before Uncle Sam takes his share of your hard-earned money, you can put a portion of your earnings to work for your future and avoid current taxation on those deposits. I often like to ask people, if you could get an interest-free loan from the government and you didn't have to pay it back until you were 71, would you take it? Would you take just some of that loan or take as much as you could get?

What would you do? I have yet to meet anyone who has said they would not take the interest-free loan.

This tax-advantaged (pretax) payroll deduction feature is one of the most powerful wealth creation tools, and it's only available through your 401(k) plan (and/or other tax-qualified retirement plans). For example, you could invest $2,000 in your 401(k) plan, and it would only cost you approximately $1,400 out of your take-home pay! What would be even better is to invest $10,000 and only give up the use of approximately $7,000* from your take-home pay. That's a $3,000 interest-free loan from Uncle Sam. Not too shabby!

*Assumes a 30 percent combined federal and state income tax rate. Your tax rates may vary.

The primary stipulation that Uncle Sam imposes in order for you to receive this tax benefit is that you don't draw on the funds until you reach age 59½. When you draw the funds from your 401(k), they will be taxed as ordinary income. If you withdraw funds from your 401(k) before reaching age 59½, you will have to pay a 10 percent penalty on top of the income tax in most cases. That's like paying the bank a penalty for prepaying an interest-free loan! The full scope of tax rules affecting your 401(k) is discussed in chapter 8.

RULE #2:
BLEND IN MORE ROTH CONTRIBUTIONS OVER TIME WITHOUT REDUCING YOUR PERCENTAGE OF SALARY CONTRIBUTED.

There is now a second and potentially more valuable tax-planning tool called the Roth 401(k). This option allows you to invest your savings compensation after it is taxed but avoid taxation on all funds when you withdraw them during your financial freedom years. Consider the effect of being taxed on the seed and being able to reap the harvest tax-free! This can be particularly valuable for long-term investors, as the earnings on your investments can be far greater than the amount invested (see Aunt Gladys's story). Not only would you potentially pay tax on a smaller amount of income, but also Roth 401(k) assets have other valuable tax benefits that can help you reduce taxation on Social Security income or on your estate after death. The difficulty with Roth contributions is that you don't get the current tax deduction, thus making it harder to build up your assets. The good news is you can choose to do both pretax contributions and Roth simultaneously. I advise plan participants who have yet to build up substantial assets that it is more important to build wealth than to worry about how it will be taxed. Once you've built up assets, you should then begin to focus more on tax reduction strategies. One such strategy would be to start investing a portion of your 401(k) contributions under the Roth election option in your plan. Try to do this without reducing the gross amount you contribute.

ROTH VS. TRADITIONAL 401(K)

401(k) Type	Age	Payroll Deduction Amount	Tax Savings Rate	Net After-tax Outlay*	Accum. Value** at Age 67	After-tax** Income for 20 years	After-tax** Income for 25 years
Traditional	37	$10,000	30%	$7,000	$790,581	$42,292	$37,395
Roth	37	$7,000	-0-	$7,000	$553,407	$42,292	$37,395
Roth	37	$10,000	-0-	$10,000	$790,581	$60,417	$53,422
Traditional	37	$7,500	30%	$5,250	$592,936	$31,719	$28,047
Roth	37	$5,250	-0-	$5,250	$415,055	$31,719	$28,047
Roth	37	$7,500	-0-	$7,500	$592,936	$45,313	$40,066

*Assumes a 30 percent blended income tax rate during all years.
**The table above assumes a 6 percent rate of return during accumulation phase, a 5 percent rate of return during distribution phase. This is not intended to represent any particular investment, nor is this a recommendation for an investment. These returns are not guaranteed. Your results may vary.

What this table shows is that it is much easier on your paycheck to contribute to the traditional 401(k) (pre-tax) than it is to contribute to a Roth 401(k) (after-tax). In order for you to reach an annual contribution of $10,000 under the traditional method, you only have to give up $7,000 from your take home pay, compliments of Uncle Sam and his interest free loan on the taxes normally due. The table also shows that if you contribute the same after-tax amount to a Roth account as you would have taken from your net pay under the traditional method, there is no increased income benefit by contributing into a Roth versus traditional 401(k) account. This assumes that your tax bracket doesn't increase during your financial independence. There are, however, other tax advantages that Roth may provide, relative to your Social Security benefits and your overall tax rate. If your tax bracket is higher during your financial freedom years, then Roth would be advantageous. However, if your tax bracket is lower in your later years, the traditional method could turn out better.

In summary, *the smart investor has money invested in both*. If you can reach your savings compensation target and hold that level regardless of tax treatment (pretax vs. after-tax), then blending in a good portion of Roth contributions will most likely add to your net income during financial freedom. Use Roth contributions wisely.

RULE #3:
INVEST A PERCENTAGE OF SALARY, NOT A FLAT DOLLAR AMOUNT.

Later in this chapter, I discuss that one of the benefits of a 401(k) is the payroll deduction and how you only have to make the decision to save once and then forget it. This becomes particularly important over time as your income increases and you proceed to increase your standard of living. At this point, it would be dangerous for you to forget that even higher wage earners have to lay away a proportionate part of their working machine output to afford the right Personal Retirement Machine. The portion of your earnings that represent savings compensation is virtually the same regardless of how much you make. It's easy to underestimate the psychological effect of changes in standard of living. The fact is that you identify yourself in many ways with your lifestyle, and when you plan for financial freedom, you'll need a retirement machine built to sustain that lifestyle.

In keeping with making the decision once and adapting your finances over time, it is critical that as your pay increases, your 401(k) savings amount increases as well. *Therefore, electing a percentage of your pay for payroll deduction is the best method to help you stay on track.* This of course doesn't mean you shouldn't increase that percentage over time as your discretionary income increases with higher earnings; you should make every effort to increase it. Think of it as taking money from one pocket and putting it into another pocket. Even better, the money in the new pocket actually goes to work for you to create more money even while you're sleeping! *Would you rather work for money or have money work for you?*

RULE #4:
USE DOLLAR COST AVERAGING, AND NEVER STOP CONTRIBUTING.

Payroll deduction also has a more important effect on your ability to succeed. This is called dollar cost averaging (DCA). Dollar cost averaging is the practice by which a person invests a like amount each period (such as weekly or monthly) into the same investment or group of investments over a long period of time. The effect is that DCA provides you with the ability to automatically buy more shares when prices are down and fewer shares when prices are up. This provides 401(k) investors with the potential advantage of lowering the average buy price for shares in their investments if they maintain a consistent savings level. This power to provide investors with a potentially lower average buy price for their shares is why it is among the most important of the seven rules.

In order to take full advantage of dollar cost averaging, you must *never stop contributing.* One of the biggest mistakes people make is to stop contributing when the markets do poorly. I can assure you that as difficult as it is to buy into a downward market, those disciplined investors who do so are more likely to recover faster during the following recovery than those who don't. The primary reason this may hold true is that, by dollar cost averaging, consistent investors buy shares of mutual funds and exchange traded funds at low prices when the markets are down and have the potential to realize greater profits on those lower priced shares as the market recovers. Exchange traded funds and index funds are the cornerstone of successful dollar cost averaging, because the holdings in those funds rarely change.

Investing in an index such as the S&P 500, along with a variety of other stock and bond market indices, is a common way to build a diversified portfolio. There are multitudes of index funds designed to represent the various market indices, including the S&P Mid Cap 400 Index, the Russell 2000 Index, the MSCI EAFE (Europe & Asia) Index, the Barclays Aggregate Bond Index, and many more. These portfolios eliminate active management and simply invest in the group of stocks or bonds that make up an index in a similar allocation to that of the index. While your performance may vary and future results are not guaranteed, diversification and dollar cost averaging may help mitigate the effects of market declines over longer periods of time. So let me reiterate, *never stop contributing!*

ACTION ITEM

If you are not familiar with exchange traded funds (ETFs), make an effort to learn about them and review the basic differences between mutual funds and ETFs, including investment management costs. Examples of ETFs are the SPDR S&P 500 Dividend fund (symbol SDY) and the iShares Mid Cap 400 Index (symbol IJH). ETFs will be an important element in your dollar cost averaging strategy.

Check to see whether ETFs are available as investment options in your 401(k) plan. If they aren't, ask your employer to add them.

RULE #5:
DIVERSIFY, DIVERSIFY, DIVERSIFY,
AND REBALANCE.

Among the most valuable keys to successful long-term investing, diversification can be the most important. *While time is your ally, diversification is your best friend!* I say this because time is passive and constant. You either use it, or you lose it. It doesn't step up and save you when you need it most like when markets are crashing. Proper diversification can help you in those times when certain investment markets are unfavorable.

Most people think that having mutual funds diversifies them. They further think that by having three or four of them they are well diversified. I would say that diversification is much more complex than that and that the majority of people do not have an optimal portfolio allocation. Many people simply aren't diversified, and that leaves them more vulnerable to volatility and shifts in the investment markets.

We have developed a series of what we consider optimal asset allocation models designed for various investment styles ranging from aggressive to ultraconservative. We explore these in greater detail in chapter 7. The number of mutual fund and/or ETF (exchange traded fund) holdings in these allocations ranges from 7 to 12 different holdings based on the investment style. These portfolios offer investors a way to be properly diversified even without having to keep track of the various investment sectors, and/or how they perform during various economic cycles. It is important to understand that over time, through various economic and socioeconomic cycles, different investment sectors will rise up to be the top performers. Because these trends are developed based on the current economic environment, *this year's top-performing sector could be next year's worst.* The fact is, that scenario is not unusual.

The value of diversification is that if you allocate assets to virtually all investment sectors, you will always have money in the best performing sectors. This fundamental fact may allow you to offset some or all of the declines in poor-performing markets with potential gains from the best-performing market segments.

Another important consideration in favor of a well-diversified portfolio is that an investor can remain confident in their strategy when markets are shaky and avoid rash emotional decisions. Decisions based on emotions such as fear and anxiety may backfire. This often increases the risk level in a portfolio and may cause irreversible damage to your long-term average returns. The value of proper portfolio allocation is that you avoid doing what most human beings are prone to do—sell when values are low and buy when markets are high. This is because most emotionally based investment decisions are usually wrong, very wrong! We address specific asset allocation strategies in chapter 7.

A key component of getting the most out of your diversification is *rebalancing*. Rebalancing is when you reduce or increase positions in your portfolio periodically, such as annually, to return them to the same percentage allocation you set out with at the beginning of that year. The effect is that you sell some of your highest growth investments (take profits) and buy some additional shares in the slower growth or even poorer performing investment sectors (buy low). Keep in mind that it is not unreasonable to believe that the weakest performers this year could turn out to be the best performers next year and vice versa. Did you ever hear the Wall Street saying "buy low and sell high?" That's exactly what rebalancing does!

Most 401(k) plans offer some type of automatic rebalancing feature. You will, however, have to make an election to have it done. Some plans may offer automatic rebalancing for certain managed portfolios, while others may offer a rebalancing service for any allocation you choose. You will also need to select the timing of the rebalancing—quarterly, semiannually, or annually. I recommend *annual rebalancing*.

ACTION ITEM

Investigate your employer's 401(k) plan to determine what type of rebalancing services and features are available. If you are investing in an asset allocation model portfolio, check to see that rebalancing is done automatically and make the rebalancing frequency annual. If you are choosing your own investment allocation, seek the advice of a financial advisor to assure proper balance and add the annual rebalancing feature to your account.

While past performance is not a guarantee of future performance, and I cannot promise you that your results will be the same as Aunt Gladys's (see "The Power of Compounding"), I can say that long-term investments hold the best possibility of positive returns. There are many reasons why Aunt Gladys's story is so relevant here. In fact, it's profound in that her story represents a simple yet powerful point regarding the fundamental truths in successful long-term investing and 401(k) plans: be patient.

RULE #6:
BE PATIENT. PATIENCE COMES TO THOSE WHO WAIT.

Time is your ally. However, time will only be your ally should you elect to be patient. One of my favorite proverbs is "patience comes to those who wait." The point being it doesn't take a lot of effort to be patient, just self-control. The second key point is that you need to keep contributing throughout all of the market cycles. When you think of the potential illustrated by Aunt Gladys's story, one might imagine that investing $2,000 or more every year for 30 years could create a much larger nest egg. Then consider the effect of increasing your annual contribution every year as your income rises, and now you have a way to combat inflation. If your employer either matches or contributes to your plan through profit sharing, that will dramatically increase your savings potential. You can now begin to see that buying your own Personal Retirement Machine is within your reach.

401(k) plans and other employer-sponsored retirement plans provide employees with a variety of tools and features to make successful investing even easier than it was for Aunt Gladys. Let's review these tools and their importance. You've probably heard that the payroll deduction feature of 401(k) plans is a valuable tool. Have you ever considered just how important that really is? Let's not underestimate the human factor, which is that without forced savings, many people simply wouldn't do it. Even those people who do elect to save would most likely not save with the kind of consistency required to be truly successful. Payroll deduction enables people to make the decision to save once and then forget about it as opposed to being required to cognitively decide to divert cash from their pocket to a savings account over and over again. Most people would agree that even among the most committed savers, there will be months—a lot of months—that are missed for one reason or another.

RULE #7:
NEVER TAKE WITHDRAWALS.

In keeping with the fact that time is your ally, it stands to reason that withdrawing or borrowing money from your 401(k) would counteract the beneficial effects of time. There may be circumstances that justify taking a loan from your 401(k), but taking a withdrawal is the worst thing you can do. The effect of taking a withdrawal is equivalent to a prepayment of your interest-free loan from Uncle Sam as well as a reversal of some of the value of your long-term savings efforts. When you borrow from your 401(k), you at least have the ability to pay it back on very favorable terms. When you take a withdrawal, you must pay any taxes due and possibly pay a 10 percent penalty if you're under age 59½ and you cannot redeposit that money back into the 401(k). Just think of the effect on Aunt Gladys's mutual fund savings if even 20 years after she put her $2,000 away she took a withdrawal of her original principal. That withdrawal would have reduced her value to $89,448 based on the investment returns in the S&P 500 Index over the next ten years. That represents a loss of $10,552 for a $2,000 withdrawal. *Never take withdrawals.*

ACTION STRATEGY

Follow these Seven Rules for Successful Retirement Investing:

1. Take advantage of Uncle Sam's interest-free loans.

2. Blend in more Roth contributions over time without reducing the percentage of Salary contributed.

3. Invest a percentage of salary, not a flat dollar amount.

4. Use dollar cost averaging, and never stop contributing.

5. Diversify, diversify, diversify, and rebalance

6. Be patient. Patience comes to those who wait.

7. Never take withdrawals.

The Dow Jones Industrial Average is a price-weighted index of 30 actively traded blue-chip stocks.

The NASDAQ Composite is a market-weighted index of all over-the-counter common stocks traded on the NASDAQ system.

The S&P 500 is a market capitalization weighted index of common stocks.

The Russell 2000 measures the performance of the 2,000 smallest companies in the Russell 3000 index.

The MSCI EAFE Index was created by Morgan Stanley Capital International (MSCI) and serves as a benchmark of the performance in major international equity markets as represented by 21 major MSCI indices from Europe, Australia, and Southeast Asia.

Keep in mind that investing involves risk, including the risk of loss. Investment decisions should be based on an individual's own goals, time horizon, and tolerance for risk.

Diversification does not assure an investor a profit, nor does it protect against market loss.

CHAPTER 6

BUILDING YOUR PERSONAL RETIREMENT MACHINE

You've probably heard the term, "no pain, no gain," right? Well consider this; "no commitment, no retirement." In order to appreciate fully the value of doing what it takes to build wealth and achieve financial freedom, one must first delve into the imagination. Have you ever dreamt of winning the lottery? Sure, it's pie in the sky, but it is possible. It happens to people every week. You've also probably told yourself that if you don't buy a ticket you don't have any chance to win; it could never happen. So you buy a lottery ticket every so often, or maybe even every week, hoping that one day it will pay off. Does that sound familiar? You picture yourself lying on the beach somewhere in the Caribbean with a little umbrella stuck in your drink, a good book in your hands, and the sound of waves crashing onto the sand. You envision your dream home with a big beautiful kitchen, the most awesome man cave, and/or a home entertainment room with all the latest technology. All this is in your hands, and you're financially set for the rest of your life. You never have to work again or listen to your boss give orders. You can travel to wherever your heart desires and buy the car or boat that you've always wanted. Your friends will all wish they could be as lucky as you.

If there were a method or a system that you could employ that would increase your chances of finding the winning lottery ticket, would you be interested in learning it? Once you knew how it worked, how far would you be willing to go to follow that system and take advantage of the potential results? If it involved buying something to invest in this system and you could finance it over time, would you make the payments in order to someday realize your dream? If there were a proven method to make this dream a likelihood rather than pie in the sky, what would you be willing to give up for it? All in all, what's it worth to have the ability to live the lifestyle you've always dreamed of?

Having your own, fully funded Personal Retirement Machine (PRM) could have a similar value to winning the lottery. Based on the amount you've accumulated in your PRM, you can receive a check every week or every month for a long period of time, possibly the rest of your life and your spouse's life.

With this in mind, think of what you would be willing to do to execute this technique to realize your dream. There's a feeling in your soul that this is truly within your reach. There's a very tangible feeling in your heart that achieving financial freedom and buying your own PRM is something you can and will do. You remind yourself that if you really want something in this world you can get it; all you need is the right plan of action and a commitment to make it happen. It's truly worth the effort. Reaching the point where you can declare financial independence is living this dream. It feels just like winning the lottery. It's the power to spend your days doing just the things that you like to do and never having to worry about how to afford it. It's a life where you never have to take orders from your boss again, because you no longer have a boss.

Well, not a boss who is also your employer, anyway.

Obviously, to acquire a machine that can do this for you would cost a lot of money. Everyone wants to be able to have a PRM, so there certainly isn't a shortage of demand. It's safe to say that such financial power would be worth paying some dues for. Often when I speak to people about numbers such as $750,000, $1,000,000, or even $2,000,000, they roll their eyes as if it's some grandiose scheme to believe one could amass such a large sum of money. While those amounts certainly aren't "chump change," to achieve financial freedom you will need to build significant wealth of that magnitude or more—similar to the amount you might win if you had the winning ticket in the lottery.

So in a way, what we're talking about is *a way to create your own lottery in which you're the only player, there's only one ticket, and you own it.* It's something that you can truly count on having instead of just having a one in ten million chance.

Nothing in life is impossible to achieve. If you really want to accomplish or obtain something in this world, you can find a way to do it. It's just like buying that new house or car you've always wanted; once you get over the sticker shock, you begin to review the options and come up with an affordable payment plan to achieve your objective. Will there be some sticker shock associated with the initial price for your Personal Money Machine? I will be surprised if there isn't. However, we will press on and find a way to acquire it anyway.

I've written about why a Personal Retirement Machine is something we all want and need. I think it's reasonable to believe that having a PRM is worth every penny it takes to invest into it. I've touched on some of the fundamental rules for successful investing for your financial freedom. I've also identified the tools within your 401(k)/403b plan that are available to assist with your objective. With the understanding that this process requires a commitment on your part to doing all that is necessary to be successful, let's identify the numbers that you should be thinking of when planning your 401(k) contributions and what it will take for you to create your own PRM.

When considering the amount of money you'll need to procure a PRM, you'll need to know what your allowable withdrawal rate will be. In other words, when you reach financial freedom and begin to receive payments from your PRM, you'll need to know what percentage of your nest egg you can draw out every year and be confident that you'll never run out of money for the rest of your life.

There has been much study about this withdrawal rate given different economic cycles and investment return factors. Many financial experts will say that a 4 percent withdrawal rate is the maximum in order to assure that you never exhaust your PRM assets. There have also been calculations that show that as much as a 5 percent withdrawal rate can be successful in the majority of circumstances. However, I can say that virtually every financial expert would agree that any withdrawal rate higher than 5 percent would likely result in a person running out of money well before they die.

If we establish a 5 percent withdrawal rate as our benchmark, *a PRM worth $1,000,000 would provide an annual income of approximately $50,000 per year.*

You will then need to consider how your PRM will increase your income over time to account for inflation. If you can accomplish an annual return of at least 6 percent on the money in your PRM during your financial freedom years, your PRM can increase your annual income by 3 percent each year to account for inflation and continue paying you for 30 years. By setting the dial for the PRM to increase your income by only 2 percent per year, you can extend the payout period to 38 years of inflation-adjusted income. In this example, if your target age for financial independence were 65, the PRM would provide income to you through age 95 or 103, depending on your inflation adjustment rate. The tables below show a retirement plan savings balance of $1 million as of the owners' desired age to declare financial freedom and the effect of an approximate 5 percent initial withdrawal amount that is increased annually to adjust for inflation. Given that there is a risk that a 5 percent withdrawal rate would fail to enable you to maintain a lifetime income, we will establish a set of equations to illustrate the various levels of savings compensation required for a lower withdrawal rate given various projected investment results.

As you approach financial freedom, you will want your PRM to provide an income equal to approximately 50 percent of your annual earned income from the latest years of your working career. We anticipate that Social Security will provide 20 to 25 percent[2] of your income to bring your total financial freedom income in line with our 70 percent rule of thumb. Therefore, if your income is $100,000

---

2 This is a general estimate. The higher your income, the lower the percentage of your salary that you will receive from Social Security and vice versa.

when you declare financial freedom, you'll want your PRM to provide $50,000 per year (inflation adjusted) for at least 30 years. We will construct mathematical schedules that illustrate the effect on your PRM savings balance based on a 5 percent withdrawal rate and how much you'll need to have saved in order to buy your PRM.

In the simplest of terms, your PRM will cost approximately 20 times your desired financial freedom income. The numbers will show that, in this case, your PRM will cost $1,000,000 for the standard model, which is 20 times the amount of your initial income need (20 x $50,000 = $1,000,000). In contrast, if your withdrawal rate were only 4 percent, your PRM would cost 25 times your desired financial freedom income. A simple equation that you can use to determine the amount of money needed to fund your PRM at any withdrawal rate would be as follows: your income need (i) divided by your intended withdrawal rate (wr) will equal the amount needed to fund your PRM ($). i/wr = $. Let's test this out.

You have a need for $50,000 per year of income to meet your financial freedom objective. You're thinking you can draw down based on a 5 percent withdrawal rate. How much will you need to fund your PRM?

$$\frac{50,000}{.05} = \$1,000,000$$

Keep in mind that your income will rise over time, so if you're 45 years old now and earning $50,000, there's a good chance you'll be earning in the range of $100,000 by the time you're ready to declare financial freedom. In that case, your income need from your PRM would be $50,000 (50 percent of your earned income). PRM Distribution Schedule #1 illustrates an initial income distribution of

$49,017 and an annual increase in income of 3 percent per year to account for inflation. This schedule also assumes a 6 percent annual rate of return on the underlying investments in the PRM.

PRM DISTRIBUTION SCHEDULE #1

Spend 30 years in retirement

Amount saved at time of retirement = $ 1,000,000.00

Annual interest rate = 6 percent (compounded annually)

Annual inflation rate = 3 percent

Withdraw $ 49,017.02 (in 2013 dollars) at the beginning of each year.

Age	Beginning Balance	Withdrawal Amount	Earnings	Remaining
65	$ 1,000,000.00	$ 49,017.02	$ 57,058.98	$ 1,008,041.96
66	$ 1,008,041.96	$ 50,487.53	$ 57,453.27	$ 1,015,007.70
67	$ 1,015,007.70	$ 52,002.15	$ 57,780.33	$ 1,020,785.88
68	$ 1,020,785.88	$ 53,562.22	$ 58,033.42	$ 1,025,257.08
69	$ 1,025,257.08	$ 55,169.08	$ 58,205.28	$ 1,028,293.28
70	$ 1,028,293.28	$ 56,824.16	$ 58,288.15	$ 1,029,757.27
71	$ 1,029,757.27	$ 58,528.88	$ 58,273.70	$ 1,029,502.09
72	$ 1,029,502.09	$ 60,284.75	$ 58,153.04	$ 1,027,370.39
73	$ 1,027,370.39	$ 62,093.29	$ 57,916.63	$ 1,023,193.72
74	$ 1,023,193.72	$ 63,956.09	$ 57,554.26	$ 1,016,791.89
75	$ 1,016,791.89	$ 65,874.77	$ 57,055.03	$ 1,007,972.15
76	$ 1,007,972.15	$ 67,851.01	$ 56,407.27	$ 996,528.40
77	$ 996,528.40	$ 69,886.54	$ 55,598.51	$ 982,240.37
78	$ 982,240.37	$ 71,983.14	$ 54,615.43	$ 964,872.66

Age	Beginning Balance	Withdrawal Amount	Earnings	Remaining
79	$ 964,872.66	$ 74,142.64	$ 53,443.80	$ 944,173.83
80	$ 944,173.83	$ 76,366.91	$ 52,068.41	$ 919,875.33
81	$ 919,875.33	$ 78,657.92	$ 50,473.04	$ 891,690.45
82	$ 891,690.45	$ 81,017.66	$ 48,640.37	$ 859,313.16
83	$ 859,313.16	$ 83,448.19	$ 46,551.90	$ 822,416.87
84	$ 822,416.87	$ 85,951.64	$ 44,187.91	$ 780,653.14
85	$ 780,653.14	$ 88,530.18	$ 41,527.38	$ 733,650.34
86	$ 733,650.34	$ 91,186.09	$ 38,547.85	$ 681,012.10
87	$ 681,012.10	$ 93,921.67	$ 35,225.43	$ 622,315.86
88	$ 622,315.86	$ 96,739.32	$ 31,534.59	$ 557,111.13
89	$ 557,111.13	$ 99,641.50	$ 27,448.18	$ 484,917.80
90	$ 484,917.80	$ 102,630.75	$ 22,937.22	$ 405,224.28
91	$ 405,224.28	$ 105,709.67	$ 17,970.88	$ 317,485.48
92	$ 317,485.48	$ 108,880.96	$ 12,516.27	$ 221,120.79
93	$ 221,120.79	$ 112,147.39	$ 6,538.40	$ 115,511.81
94	$ 115,511.81	$ 115,511.81	$ 0	$ 0
Totals		**$ 2,332,004.94**	**$ 1,332,004.94**	

As you can see in Schedule #1, the $1,000,000 PRM is able to pay income based on an initial distribution rate of 4.9 percent and an assumed annual earnings rate of 6 percent. In subsequent years the income increases by 3 percent per year, for 29 more years, for a total of 30 years of payments and $2,332,004 in total income. You can also see that it doesn't take long before the amount of your annual income exceeds the annual earnings on the underlying investments.

This is a very important point to recognize in an income distribution plan.

Once the net amount of earnings is less than the income being distributed from your PRM, the remaining PRM balance will begin to decline upon distributions, and that decline will accelerate each year. The result is that in year seven, the remaining balance in your PRM begins to decline. After the 30th year, the balance is zero. This of course assumes that you continue to increase your annual income throughout the 30-year period by the same percentage.

There is good reason to question whether or not a straight line percentage increase in income is necessary to account for inflation. The reason for this question is that in your later years of financial freedom, your spending habits will change and the amount of income needed (in todays' dollars) will likely decrease. It is quite common for a person or a couple to spend the most during their initial years of financial freedom and see their spending levels go down considerably as they reach older ages. This is when you may buy new cars, vacation property, or boats that you've always wanted or do the most traveling. Once we have made all of these purchases and checked off many of the items on our "bucket list," our spending needs go down. As we reach older ages, we may not be as active as we were in our 60s and 70s. Therefore, we may travel less and buy fewer new things in favor of simply spending more time with family and grandchildren. Recognizing this reality of human nature will allow you to plan for a lesser trajectory of increases in your income. It could potentially allow the PRM to continue to provide income longer based on these adjustments. Essentially, a PRM can continue to provide for longer periods at the discretion of the owner.

In PRM Distribution Schedule #2 we examine the effect of having a reduced rate of return of 5 percent on the underlying PRM assets while maintaining a similar income distribution. The result is that, with the lower investment returns, your PRM can only produce income for approximately 25 years. This risk of a lower return is a big part of reasoning that a 5 percent withdrawal rate may result in exhausting your PRM assets before you die. This scenario also illustrates how important it is to maintain a reasonable withdrawal rate and to find investments that may offer reliable income distributions. We will address this issue further in developing distribution strategies to stabilize the income from your PRM.

PRM DISTRIBUTION SCHEDULE #2

Spend 25.5 years in retirement

Amount needed at time of retirement = $ 1,000,000.00

Annual interest rate = 5 percent (compounded annually)

Annual inflation rate = 3 percent

Amount withdrawn at the beginning

of each year = $ 49,017.00 (in 2013 dollars)

Age	Beginning Balance	Withdrawal Amount	Earnings	Remaining
65	$ 1,000,000.00	$ 49,017.00	$ 47,549.15	$ 998,532.15
66	$ 998,532.15	$ 50,487.51	$ 47,402.23	$ 995,446.87
67	$ 995,446.87	$ 52,002.14	$ 47,172.24	$ 990,616.97
68	$ 990,616.97	$ 53,562.20	$ 46,852.74	$ 983,907.51
69	$ 983,907.51	$ 55,169.07	$ 46,436.92	$ 975,175.37

Age	Beginning Balance	Withdrawal Amount	Earnings	Remaining
70	$ 975,175.37	$ 56,824.14	$ 45,917.56	$ 964,268.79
71	$ 964,268.79	$ 58,528.86	$ 45,287.00	$ 951,026.93
72	$ 951,026.93	$ 60,284.73	$ 44,537.11	$ 935,279.31
73	$ 935,279.31	$ 62,093.27	$ 43,659.30	$ 916,845.35
74	$ 916,845.35	$ 63,956.07	$ 42,644.46	$ 895,533.74
75	$ 895,533.74	$ 65,874.75	$ 41,482.95	$ 871,141.94
76	$ 871,141.94	$ 67,850.99	$ 40,164.55	$ 843,455.50
77	$ 843,455.50	$ 69,886.52	$ 38,678.45	$ 812,247.43
78	$ 812,247.43	$ 71,983.12	$ 37,013.22	$ 777,277.52
79	$ 777,277.52	$ 74,142.61	$ 35,156.75	$ 738,291.66
80	$ 738,291.66	$ 76,366.89	$ 33,096.24	$ 695,021.01
81	$ 695,021.01	$ 78,657.90	$ 30,818.16	$ 647,181.27
82	$ 647,181.27	$ 81,017.63	$ 28,308.18	$ 594,471.82
83	$ 594,471.82	$ 83,448.16	$ 25,551.18	$ 536,574.84
84	$ 536,574.84	$ 85,951.61	$ 22,531.16	$ 473,154.40
85	$ 473,154.40	$ 88,530.15	$ 19,231.21	$ 403,855.45
86	$ 403,855.45	$ 91,186.06	$ 15,633.47	$ 328,302.86
87	$ 328,302.86	$ 93,921.64	$ 11,719.06	$ 246,100.28
88	$ 246,100.28	$ 96,739.29	$ 7,468.05	$ 156,829.04
89	$ 156,829.04	$ 99,641.47	$ 2,859.38	$ 60,046.95
90	$ 60,046.95	$ 60,046.95	$0	$0
Totals		$ 1,847,170.71	$ 847,170.71	

PRM Schedule #3 illustrates that one way we can resolve the reduced years of income caused by lower returns on PRM assets is to reduce the incremental increase in income from 3 percent per year to 2 percent annually. While it is important to account for inflation in our income plan, it is my opinion that, for the purpose of an initial calculation, the 2 percent annual increase may be sufficient. When you consider that after the first third of your financial freedom years, your spending levels will most likely gradually decline as you make your way into your later years. In this scenario, your PRM once again provides income for 30 years of financial freedom.

PRM WITHDRAWAL SCHEDULE #3

Spend 30 years in retirement

Amount saved at time of retirement = $ 1,000,000.00

Annual interest rate = 5 percent (compounded annually)

Annual inflation rate = 2 percent

Withdraw $ 49,185.46 (in 2013 dollars) at the beginning of each year

$0 will be left in your account (purchasing power of $0 in 2013)

Age	Beginning Balance	Withdrawal Amount	Earnings	Remaining
65	$ 1,000,000.00	$ 49,185.46	$ 47,540.73	$ 998,355.27
66	$ 998,355.27	$ 50,169.17	$ 47,409.31	$ 995,595.41
67	$ 995,595.41	$ 51,172.55	$ 47,221.14	$ 991,644.00
68	$ 991,644.00	$ 52,196.00	$ 46,972.40	$ 986,420.39
69	$ 986,420.39	$ 53,239.92	$ 46,659.02	$ 979,839.50
70	$ 979,839.50	$ 54,304.72	$ 46,276.74	$ 971,811.51
71	$ 971,811.51	$ 55,390.82	$ 45,821.03	$ 962,241.73
72	$ 962,241.73	$ 56,498.63	$ 45,287.16	$ 951,030.26

Age	Beginning Balance	Withdrawal Amount	Earnings	Remaining
73	$ 951,030.26	$ 57,628.60	$ 44,670.08	$ 938,071.74
74	$ 938,071.74	$ 58,781.18	$ 43,964.53	$ 923,255.09
75	$ 923,255.09	$ 59,956.80	$ 43,164.91	$ 906,463.20
76	$ 906,463.20	$ 61,155.94	$ 42,265.36	$ 887,572.63
77	$ 887,572.63	$ 62,379.05	$ 41,259.68	$ 866,453.25
78	$ 866,453.25	$ 63,626.64	$ 40,141.33	$ 842,967.95
79	$ 842,967.95	$ 64,899.17	$ 38,903.44	$ 816,972.22
80	$ 816,972.22	$ 66,197.15	$ 37,538.75	$ 788,313.82
81	$ 788,313.82	$ 67,521.09	$ 36,039.64	$ 756,832.36
82	$ 756,832.36	$ 68,871.52	$ 34,398.04	$ 722,358.89
83	$ 722,358.89	$ 70,248.95	$ 32,605.50	$ 684,715.44
84	$ 684,715.44	$ 71,653.93	$ 30,653.08	$ 643,714.59
85	$ 643,714.59	$ 73,087.00	$ 28,531.38	$ 599,158.96
86	$ 599,158.96	$ 74,548.74	$ 26,230.51	$ 550,840.73
87	$ 550,840.73	$ 76,039.72	$ 23,740.05	$ 498,541.06
88	$ 498,541.06	$ 77,560.51	$ 21,049.03	$ 442,029.58
89	$ 442,029.58	$ 79,111.72	$ 18,145.89	$ 381,063.74
90	$ 381,063.74	$ 80,693.96	$ 15,018.49	$ 315,388.28
91	$ 315,388.28	$ 82,307.84	$ 11,654.02	$ 244,734.46
92	$ 244,734.46	$ 83,953.99	$ 8,039.02	$ 168,819.49
93	$ 168,819.49	$ 85,633.07	$ 4,159.32	$ 87,345.74
94	$ 87,345.74	$ 87,345.74	$ 0	$ 0
Totals		$ 1,995,359.59	$ 995,359.59	

In designing your PRM income plan, another important consideration would be the benefit of lowering the annual increase amount to 2 percent even while earning the original 6 percent projected rate of return. In this scenario, you would be able to continue receiving income from your PRM for over 38 years. This would be a viable consideration for those of you who wish to become financially independent at a younger age, such as 60 or younger. Should that be your goal, it's important to keep in mind that your need for income will be over a much longer period than the average person.

When you're planning for longer periods of financial freedom, it becomes more difficult to design a PRM to meet your needs. This is due to what is called *longevity risk*. Longevity risk is the possibility of running out of money during your lifetime. This risk increases the longer you live or when you plan for longer periods of financial freedom. Therefore, the standard model PRM is designed to produce income for a period of 30 years to minimize longevity risk. Consider the possible life expectancies of a husband and wife who reach age 65. Based on a study prepared by Actuarial Consultants Inc. in 2012, there's a *50 percent chance* that one spouse will live to age 91 and a *25 percent chance* that at least one spouse will live beyond age 95. There is also a *10 percent chance* that one of the spouses will live beyond age 98. As a result, those people beginning financial freedom at age 65, 66, or 67 will need to have a PRM to cover at least a 30-year period, and people choosing to begin at a younger age may need their PRM to produce income for 35 years or longer.

Someone who leaves the workforce early, such as age 60, would potentially need income for 35 years under this assumption. Therefore, you need a more careful approach in designing your PRM to stretch your income over a long time frame. The lower increase rate also helps account for those years where investment returns may be lower than anticipated.

Keep in mind that poor portfolio performance can adversely affect the amount you can withdraw from your PRM.

Finally, we look at PRM Distribution Schedule #4, below, which I believe more accurately reflects how your income needs will change over time considering both inflation and common trends in spending habits.

As previously mentioned, your spending habits will change over time such that your need for income (in today's dollars), will decrease in each third of your financial freedom years. I will consider each ten-year period in your life following age 65, as a third of your financial independence.

In this table, we begin with a PRM income distribution rate of 5 percent and an inflation adjustment of 3 percent. The assumption is that this person reaches financial freedom at age 65 and that their desired income/spending need will drop by 10 percent after each ten-year period. We do this by selecting a future income need in today's dollars that is ten percent below the initial need for each decade and continue to increase that need for inflation from the outset of the financial planning calculation. So if your desired income is $50,000 per year at age 65, your projected need as of age 75 will be $45,000 per year in today's dollars, which is then projected out to that point in time based on a 3 percent inflation rate. At age 85, the need would be $40,500 as we again ratchet income downward by 10 percent. However, in each case, throughout the years I continue to increase the income desired by 3 percent annually from the present value.

PRM DISTRIBUTION SCHEDULE #4

Spend 30 years in financial freedom

Amount saved at time of retirement = $ 1,000,000.00

Annual interest rate = 6% (compounded annually)

Annual inflation rate = 3%

Withdraw $ 49,017.02 (in 2015 dollars) at the beginning of each year

Age	Beginning Balance	Withdrawal Amount	Earnings	Remaining
65	$ 1,000,000.00	$ 49,017.02	$ 57,058.98	$ 1,008,041.96
66	$ 1,008,041.96	$ 50,487.53	$ 57,453.27	$ 1,015,007.70
67	$ 1,015,007.70	$ 52,002.15	$ 57,780.33	$ 1,020,785.88
68	$ 1,020,785.88	$ 53,562.22	$ 58,033.42	$ 1,025,257.08
69	$ 1,025,257.08	$ 55,169.08	$ 58,205.28	$ 1,028,293.28
70	$ 1,028,293.28	$ 56,824.16	$ 58,288.15	$ 1,029,757.27
71	$ 1,029,757.27	$ 58,528.88	$ 58,273.70	$ 1,029,502.09
72	$ 1,029,502.09	$ 60,284.75	$ 58,153.04	$ 1,027,370.39
73	$ 1,027,370.39	$ 62,093.29	$ 57,916.63	$ 1,023,193.72
74	$ 1,023,193.72	$ 63,956.09	$ 57,554.26	$ 1,016,791.89
75	$ 1,016,791.89	$ 65,874.77	$ 57,055.03	$ 1,007,972.15
76	$ 1,007,972.15	$ 67,851.01	$ 56,407.27	$ 996,528.40
77	$ 996,528.40	$ 69,886.54	$ 55,598.51	$ 982,240.37
78	$ 982,240.37	$ 71,983.14	$ 54,615.43	$ 964,872.66
79	$ 964,872.66	$ 74,142.64	$ 53,443.80	$ 944,173.83
80	$ 944,173.83	$ 76,366.91	$ 52,068.41	$ 919,875.33
81	$ 919,875.33	$ 78,657.92	$ 50,473.04	$ 891,690.45

Age	Beginning Balance	Withdrawal Amount	Earnings	Remaining
82	$ 891,690.45	$ 81,017.66	$ 48,640.37	$ 859,313.16
83	$ 859,313.16	$ 83,448.19	$ 46,551.90	$ 822,416.87
84	$ 822,416.87	$ 85,951.64	$ 44,187.91	$ 780,653.14
85	$ 780,653.14	$ 88,530.18	$ 41,527.38	$ 733,650.34
86	$ 733,650.34	$ 91,186.09	$ 38,547.85	$ 681,012.10
87	$ 681,012.10	$ 93,921.67	$ 35,225.43	$ 622,315.86
88	$ 622,315.86	$ 96,739.32	$ 31,534.59	$ 557,111.13
89	$ 557,111.13	$ 99,641.50	$ 27,448.18	$ 484,917.80
90	$ 484,917.80	$ 102,630.75	$ 22,937.22	$ 405,224.28
91	$ 405,224.28	$ 105,709.67	$ 17,970.88	$ 317,485.48
92	$ 317,485.48	$ 108,880.96	$ 12,516.27	$ 221,120.79
93	$ 221,120.79	$ 112,147.39	$ 6,538.40	$ 115,511.81
94	$ 115,511.81	$ 115,511.81	$ 0	$ 0
Totals		**$ 2,332,004.94**	**$ 1,332,004.94**	

www.MyCalculators.com

As you can see, assuming a 6 percent rate of return on the underlying assets, the PRM is able to produce income for 30 years and have a substantial remaining balance that would allow income to continue for at least three more years. This is a result of the periodic adjustment to spending. This also provides a cushion in the PRM in the event that investment returns are less than anticipated.

The risk of investment return volatility must be factored into any financial plan. However, when it comes to planning for financial freedom, accounting for unforeseen risks such as market declines is of paramount importance. Even at a 5 percent rate of return and a 3 percent inflation adjustment, the PRM is able to produce the desired income for 28 years as a result of the retraction of the income amount every ten years. This is three years longer than our initial projection based on a 5 percent growth rate.

As a rule of thumb, by planning for 10 percent lower income needs during each subsequent decade of financial freedom, your PRM will produce income for approximately three to four years longer than it would in the case of a straight line incremental increase. The assumption of lower income needs later in life is predicated on maintaining adequate health insurance coverage. Health care is likely to be one of the largest expenditures in your budget at that point in your life.

In all of these examples, we make assumptions as to the earnings rate or investment returns that you will garner over the course of time, in order to calculate a predicted outcome. In order to calculate projections so that we may have a model to create your PRM, we must use assumed rates of return. The returns used here are believed to be reasonable assumptions of long-term average returns that can be expected given a balanced, well-diversified portfolio of stocks, bonds, and conservative investments. While these may be reasonable assumptions, *there is no guarantee that any of us will receive a 6 percent or 5 percent rate of return.* For those difficult years when returns are harder to come by, it pays to have some cushion in your PRM.

It is a virtual impossibility that your investments would provide the exact same rate of return each year. Even if in your circumstance, your investment returns average exactly 6 percent, the order in which you receive those gains vs. years with losses will have an impact on your degree of success and your allowable withdrawal rate. These potential variances give rise to the need for reliable sources of income and returns from your PRM assets. The focus on *reliability of income* is reviewed in greater detail later in this book. Proper investment allocation is paramount to your success.

ACTION ITEMS

Project your pre-freedom income (your income in the years just before retirement) based on a reasonable growth rate of your income over time.

Multiply your pre-freedom income number by .5 to determine your desired income from your PRM (your financial freedom income). Then multiply your financial freedom income by 20 to determine the cost of your PRM.

Review your current asset allocation and 401(k) balances. Consider whether your current investment strategy is in line with your appropriate risk tolerance based on age and personal comfort level.

HOW MUCH WILL IT TAKE TO ACHIEVE FINANCIAL FREEDOM?

In the first section of this chapter, "Building Your Personal Retirement Machine," we established that the maximum withdrawal rate from your PRM during financial freedom will be 5 percent. Now that this is done, we can also determine the correct percentage of your current compensation that you will need to allocate as savings compensation to put toward the purchase of your own PRM.

The first step is to project what your "pre-freedom income" will be. We can simply use your last working years' income, however, if your income spikes late in your career, we would want to use an average of the last three to five years. We can make assumptions of certain growth rates for your income over time. One fairly reliable way to do this is to estimate that your income will keep pace with the cost of living. We can then project your pre-freedom income simply by growing your current income by a projected inflation rate. It is my sincere wish that your income grows faster than that. However, in today's economy that can be a challenge in and of itself. At the same time, failing to account for increases in your income and the cost of living would be a fundamental flaw in planning to have the income you need to be truly financially independent.

To help you understand the financial impact of various lifestyle, spending, and savings decisions, I will share with you the story of two lifelike scenarios of families with whom we can relate. We will examine what they have done financially to this point and what they will need to save in order to obtain their desired PRM in the future. The idea is to create a *PRM layaway plan* that has been calculated with the objective of achieving financial freedom at a projected age.

By making the suggested deposits into the layaway plan, we can reasonably expect to reach the range of our objective based on various rates of return. I will make certain assumptions herein so that I may offer real numbers that we can all work with and reasonable lifestyle scenarios. I'll be using annual incomes of $100,000 per family because it will be relatively easy to multiply or divide and recalculate the numbers to reflect your own income. For example, if you (or your household) earn $77,000 per year, you may take the dollar amounts we use in these scenarios, multiply them by .77, and arrive at a reasonably accurate number for your personal situation. If your income is $118,000 you can multiply the numbers by 1.18 to reflect your needs. Whatever your numbers are, the story will be the same and the percentage of your pay that's really "savings compensation" will be the same. The gross income number of $100,000 could represent the total household income of a husband and wife or the income of one individual.

I'll start with the story of Mike and Mary Lou Freewheeler, a married couple, both aged 37, with combined annual earnings of $100,000. Mike and Mary Lou have been married for nearly ten years and have owned their own home for the last five. They live in a beautiful seaside town where Mike grew up. They met while taking sailing classes in their early 20s. They both love the ocean and enjoy being out on the water. Sailing has become their top summertime hobby. They also enjoy snowmobiling in the winter.

The Freewheelers have a great lifestyle and have worked hard to buy the things they like. Unfortunately, prior to this point the Freewheelers were relatively poor savers, having put most of their disposable income into buying and maintaining a very nice home and buying a few extreme toys like a boat and his and her snowmobiles.

As of age 37, Mike and Mary Lou Freewheeler's combined retirement savings are $10,000. Mary Lou stopped contributing to her 401(k) shortly after they got married so they could save more money for a house. She has not gotten back into it since then. Mike contributes only a small percentage of his pay, and as a result he is not receiving the full match that his employer offers. The Freewheelers have over $10,000 in credit card debt and $30,000 in auto loans. The average interest rate on that debt is 8 percent.

The Freewheelers have an annual debt service (interest on credit) cost of approximately $3,200 (exclusive of their mortgage). They chose to buy a fairly expensive car that they really liked because they were offered a "great deal" on it. They have had a similar amount of credit card debt for the last five years since they bought their house. It seems that every month all they can do to pay the interest on the card plus cover whatever they bought that month. Unfortunately, when you use credit to buy things, there is a cost beyond the price of those goods. *Their loan interest for credit purchases of nonessential items is the annual penalty for buying things they couldn't afford in the first place* ("bad debt"). It's also money that could have been used to invest for their PRM and their future. Instead, the banks will add it to their corporate earnings.

Like many people, the Freewheelers are behind in establishing the proper savings levels for long-term financial success, and they are not on track to achieve financial freedom at their desired age. They have never been afforded an understanding of the difference between *spending compensation* and *savings compensation* or how to fund their layaway plan to procure a Personal Retirement Machine. This may be in part because they have yet to engage a financial advisor to assist them with formulating a personalized financial plan. They are not aware of the fact that part of their compensation really is savings compensation. As a result, they have established a lifestyle that is not truly affordable.

In the absence of a financial plan, we can use some common rules of thumb to determine what the Freewheelers will need to do to achieve financial freedom. To be truly financially independent, on average, a person or couple will need a program that will produce 70 percent of their working income for 30 years or longer. A reasonable assumption is that Social Security will provide approximately 20 to 25 percent of your working income. The 70 percent factor is also based on the assumption that most, if not all, of your debts are paid off and any remaining debt will be paid off in less than five years at the regular payment schedule. The first assumption is that they would want to declare financial freedom at age 67 by creating a PRM that will provide approximately 50 percent of their gross income during their most recent working years. I'll call this their "pre-freedom income."

The age at which you declare financial independence is one of the most influential factors in determining the cost of your PRM and the amount you will need to put into your PRM layaway plan. For this example, I am using age 67 in part because this is the age at which many of us will be eligible for our full Social Security benefits. Those benefits are a factor in determining what percentage of our pre-freedom income needs to be produced by our PRM. Also, the older the age you intend to declare financial independence, the lower the payments on your PRM layaway plan. Therefore, keep in mind that while the idea of "early retirement" is really nice, the required savings compensation increases with each year prior to age 67 that you select.

Given their current income of $100,000 and the assumption that their income will increase on average by *2.34 percent* per year throughout their working careers, their combined pre-freedom income will be $200,000 at age 67. Therefore, their Personal Retirement Machine will need to provide them $100,000 (*50 percent*) to maintain the family's lifestyle in retirement. The additional $40,000 (*20 percent*) needed should come from Social Security. In order for the Freewheelers to put their PRM on layaway, they will first need to calculate the target cost. They will also need help to determine what percentage of their pay should be considered savings compensation and diverted into their 401(k). This will be the percentage amount of their pay they must contribute to their 401(k) plans combined with their employer matching benefits throughout their remaining working years to achieve financial freedom. Our calculations will base these projections on the assumption that the Freewheelers investment returns will average between 7 and 8 percent annually during their working (accumulation) years. The calculation of how much the PRM can distribute as income will be based on a presumed 5 to 6 percent rate of return during their financial freedom (distribution) years.

The $10,000 question everyone has is: How much will it take to buy a PRM that will produce an inflation-adjusted income of $100,000 per year for 30 or more years?

Before we go on to the calculations, let's look at another family and a slightly different financial scenario so that we can compare the two and see how the calculations are affected by their financial history.

David and Julie Cashwell are also age 37 and have an annual income of $100,000. David and Julie became friends through work when they were 27 years old and soon after started dating. They have similar jobs and make equal pay, which was $30,000 each at age 27 and has now reached $50,000 each. Their employer offered a fairly generous 401(k) plan match back then, and they compared notes about the idea of taking advantage of that benefit. They both started contributing that same year at age 27 and have been consistent contributors ever since.

The Cashwells own and live in a modest home in Northern Massachusetts with their two children. Over the years, they have gradually improved their home through do-it-yourself projects and careful planning. They have also been advised by their financial advisor to refinance their mortgage in a timely manner to keep their interest rates low. They generally do not use credit cards, and as a result they have no debt other than their home mortgage and a small car loan. Their hobbies include skiing, hiking, and camping, and in the summer they like to visit Cape Cod.

The Cashwells will have to accumulate the same amount as the Freewheelers to procure their PRM. They will need the same percentages of pre-freedom income from their PRM and Social Security to declare financial independence. However, the amount of their income that must be considered savings compensation at this point will be quite different. Ten years ago David and Julie elected to contribute a flat dollar amount of $150 per month each ($3,600 per year combined) to their 401(k) plans and have continued with that contribution amount ever since. They also received an employer-matching contribution of 3 percent of their salary for a total of another $200 per month ($2,400 per year) on average, for a combined total of $6,000 per year in contributions. Based on earning an assumed 7 percent annual rate of return, the Cashwells have accumulated $86,542. Unfortunately, as good as the Cashwells have been at saving money, their 401(k) contributions had never increased, because when they signed up for their 401(k) plan ten years ago, they elected to contribute a flat dollar amount as opposed to a percentage of their salary. During that time, their salary has gone up by a total of nearly 67 percent. As a result, their contribution percentage as it relates to their salary was 6 percent when they started and is only 3.6 percent today. Had the Cashwells maintained the same 6 percent of pay contribution throughout the years, they would have accumulated an additional $38,062, for a total of $124,604.

In spite of this lost opportunity, I will give the Cashwells a lot of credit for managing their finances effectively. They may not have maximized their contributions to their 401(k), but they were meticulous about saving money. They were also careful to avoid excess spending and the related debt that goes along with that. The fact that they have stayed away from the use of debt to purchase things they couldn't afford is saving them thousands of dollars in interest charges every year in comparison with other families like the Freewheelers. They can now direct additional funds to their 401(k) plan in pursuit of their PRM.

If we assume that both the Cashwells and the Freewheelers are able to grow their earned income by an average of 2.34 percent per year, their income will double over the next 30 years. As a result, their pre-freedom income will be $200,000. You may recall that we want their PRM to be able to provide 50 percent of their pre-freedom income, and we expect Social Security to provide an additional 20 percent. Thus, their PRM will need to provide $100,000 per year. We can now create our first set of equations for determining the required value of our PRM.

$$PRM \times .05 = \$100,000$$

or

$$\$100,000/.05 = PRM$$

The first equation is based on the knowledge that our desired income amount to be received from the PRM is $100,000. We also know that our initial drawdown rate can only be up to 5 percent of our PRM value (see earlier in this chapter). What we still need to determine is how much we will need to have accumulated on layaway to buy/create our PRM. So this equation asks what number multiplied by 5 percent will provide us with $100,000. We can also consider the inverse of this equation, that is, to divide the desired income amount by 5 percent to determine our PRM cost/value. In other words, the financial freedom income need divided by .05 equals the total amount needed to buy your PRM.

What I like about mathematics is that there are often ways of simplifying the means to calculate your answers. We know we need 5 percent of a number, and that number is 100 percent of what we need. Whereas 5 percent goes into 100 percent 20 times, a simpler equation is to multiply the financial freedom income desired by 20, $100,000 x 20 = $2,000,000.

A good rule of thumb is that your PRM will cost 20 times your financial freedom income number.

Armed with this information, we may now embark on a quest to build and create wealth consistent with achieving the goal of financial freedom. The next step is to take what we have saved and determine what we need to add to that each month or year to accumulate our desired nest egg. This of course will also depend on an assumed rate of return on our savings. It's my belief that long-term investors with a diversified portfolio, which is allocated consistent with their long-term investment objectives, have an opportunity to earn between 7 and 8 percent as an average annual return. This also assumes that they are wise enough to seek advice in choosing their investments and that they don't make emotional or erratic decisions with their investment strategy. The table below illustrates the amount necessary for the Freewheelers and the Cashwells to save each year for the next 30 years in order to buy their PRM.

Given that both the Freewheelers and the Cashwells will both have a pre-freedom income of $200,000, their PRM will cost $2,000,000 each. The tables below illustrate how much each family will need to contribute to their respective 401(k) plans and the growth of their current savings combined with their ongoing contributions. In each case, I assume an annual increase in personal income of 2.34 percent.

Each family will have two layaway plans to consider. The first will be based on a projected return of 7 percent annually, and the second will be based on an annual return of 8 percent. In PRM Layaway Plan #1, we first examine the financial situation for the Cashwells. The table illustrates their required contribution, projected employer-matching contributions, their projected investment earnings, and the ending balance in their 401(k) plan based on an assumed rate of return of 7 percent annually.

CASHWELL PRM LAYAWAY PLAN #1
CONTRIBUTION SCHEDULE

Fund plan for 30 years

Annual income of $ 100,000.00, increasing 2.34 percent per year

Beginning balance = $ 86,542.00

You contribute 6.96 percent of salary

Your employer will contribute 3 percent of salary

Annual interest rate = 7 percent

Year #	Beginning Balance	Ann. Contrib.	ER Contrib.	Earnings	End Balance
1.	86,542.00	6,960.00	3,000.00	6,624.28	103,126.28
2.	103,126.28	7,122.86	3,070.20	7,834.85	121,154.19
3.	121,154.19	7,289.54	3,142.04	9,150.27	140,736.04
4.	140,736.04	7,460.11	3,215.57	10,578.55	161,990.27
5.	161,990.27	7,634.68	3,290.81	12,128.27	185,044.03
6.	185,044.03	7,813.33	3,367.82	13,808.68	210,033.85
7.	210,033.85	7,996.16	3,446.62	15,629.65	237,106.30
8.	237,106.30	8,183.27	3,527.27	17,601.84	266,418.68
9.	266,418.68	8,374.76	3,609.81	19,736.64	298,139.90
10.	298,139.90	8,570.73	3,694.28	22,046.31	332,451.23
11.	332,451.23	8,771.29	3,780.73	24,544.00	369,547.25
12.	369,547.25	8,976.54	3,869.20	27,243.82	409,636.80
13.	409,636.80	9,186.59	3,959.74	30,160.91	452,944.03
14.	452,944.03	9,401.55	4,052.39	33,311.53	499,709.51
15.	499,709.51	9,621.55	4,147.22	36,713.14	550,191.41
16.	550,191.41	9,846.69	4,244.26	40,384.44	604,666.82

Year #	Beginning Balance	Ann. Contrib.	ER Contrib.	Earnings	End Balance
17.	604,666.82	10,077.11	4,343.58	44,345.55	663,433.05
18.	663,433.05	10,312.91	4,445.22	48,618.01	726,809.19
19.	726,809.19	10,554.23	4,549.24	53,224.98	795,137.64
20.	795,137.64	10,801.20	4,655.69	58,191.27	868,785.80
21.	868,785.80	11,053.95	4,764.63	63,543.54	948,147.93
22.	948,147.93	11,312.61	4,876.13	69,310.38	1,033,647.05
23.	1,033,647.05	11,577.33	4,990.23	75,522.46	1,125,737.06
24.	1,125,737.06	11,848.24	5,107.00	82,212.69	1,224,904.99
25.	1,224,904.99	12,125.49	5,226.50	89,416.40	1,331,673.38
26.	1,331,673.38	12,409.22	5,348.80	97,171.48	1,446,602.88
27.	1,446,602.88	12,699.60	5,473.96	105,518.58	1,570,295.02
28.	1,570,295.02	12,996.77	5,602.06	114,501.32	1,703,395.17
29.	1,703,395.17	13,300.89	5,733.14	124,166.50	1,846,595.71
30.	1,846,595.71	13,612.13	5,867.30	134,564.33	2,000,639.47
Totals		$297,891.33	$128,401.44	$1,487,804.67	

Based on the above table projecting an assumed 7 percent annual rate of return over 30 years, the Cashwells should now consider approximately 7 percent of their salary as savings compensation and increase their respective 401(k) contributions accordingly. They will need to start contributing $580 per month from their paycheck while receiving $250 per month in matching benefits from their employer. Their payroll deduction must be set up as a percentage of salary so that as their salary increases, their contributions will increase in the same manner. These contribution levels should enable them to achieve their goal of financial freedom in 30 years at age 67 based on an assumed annual return of 7 percent.

For the Freewheelers, the amount of their salary they will need to be designated as savings compensation will be somewhat different. Their PRM Layaway Plan #1 is based on the same assumed 7 percent annual return as the Cashwells, the same incremental increase in earnings, and the same employer-matching contribution. The only difference is that the Freewheelers start their plan with $10,000 in the account, whereas the Cashwells have already saved $86,542.

FREEWHEELER PRM LAYAWAY PLAN #1 CONTRIBUTION SCHEDULE

Fund plan for 30 years

Annual income of $ 100,000.00, increasing 2.34 percent per year

Beginning balance = $ 10,000.00

Contribute 11.77 percent of salary, invested weekly

Your employer will contribute 3 percent of salary

Annual interest rate = 7 percent, compounded daily

Year #	Beginning Balance	Ann. Contrib.	ER Contrib.	Earnings	End Balance
1.	10,000.00	11,770.00	3,000.00	1,243.89	26,013.89
2.	26,013.89	12,045.42	3,070.20	2,417.05	43,546.56
3.	43,546.56	12,327.28	3,142.04	3,700.62	62,716.50
4.	62,716.50	12,615.74	3,215.57	5,103.17	83,650.98
5.	83,650.98	12,910.95	3,290.81	6,633.96	106,486.70
6.	106,486.70	13,213.06	3,367.82	8,302.89	131,370.46
7.	131,370.46	13,522.25	3,446.62	10,120.62	158,459.95
8.	158,459.95	13,838.67	3,527.27	12,098.58	187,924.47

Year #	Beginning Balance	Ann. Contrib.	ER Contrib.	Earnings	End Balance
9.	187,924.47	14,162.49	3,609.81	14,249.06	219,945.84
10.	219,945.84	14,493.90	3,694.28	16,585.25	254,719.27
11.	254,719.27	14,833.05	3,780.73	19,121.31	292,454.37
12.	292,454.37	15,180.15	3,869.20	21,872.45	333,376.16
13.	333,376.16	15,535.36	3,959.74	24,854.98	377,726.23
14.	377,726.23	15,898.89	4,052.39	28,086.43	425,763.94
15.	425,763.94	16,270.92	4,147.22	31,585.61	477,767.69
16.	477,767.69	16,651.66	4,244.26	35,372.72	534,036.34
17.	534,036.34	17,041.31	4,343.58	39,469.43	594,890.66
18.	594,890.66	17,440.08	4,445.22	43,899.00	660,674.96
19.	660,674.96	17,848.18	4,549.24	48,686.42	731,758.80
20.	731,758.80	18,265.83	4,655.69	53,858.48	808,538.79
21.	808,538.79	18,693.25	4,764.63	59,443.95	891,440.62
22.	891,440.62	19,130.67	4,876.13	65,473.70	980,921.11
23.	980,921.11	19,578.33	4,990.23	71,980.85	1,077,470.52
24.	1,077,470.52	20,036.46	5,107.00	79,000.98	1,181,614.96
25.	1,181,614.96	20,505.31	5,226.50	86,572.22	1,293,918.99
26.	1,293,918.99	20,985.14	5,348.80	94,735.53	1,414,988.46
27.	1,414,988.46	21,476.19	5,473.96	103,534.83	1,545,473.44
28.	1,545,473.44	21,978.73	5,602.06	113,017.28	1,686,071.50
29.	1,686,071.50	22,493.03	5,733.14	123,233.45	1,837,531.12
30.	1,837,531.12	23,019.37	5,867.30	134,237.62	2,000,655.41
Totals		$503,761.67	$128,401.44	$1,358,492.33	

www.MyCalculators.com

As you can see, the Freewheelers savings compensation percentage will need to be 11.77 percent. They will need to contribute $980.83 per month to their 401(k) plan while receiving $250 per month from their employers to reach their dream of financial freedom by age 67. They too must choose to have their savings deducted as a percentage of their salary so that as their income increases, their contributions will keep pace. Based on an assumed 7 percent annual growth rate, the Freewheelers will have to treat nearly 5 percent more of their current income as savings compensation than do the Cashwells.

In this next scenario, we will examine the effect of an assumed 8 percent rate of return on determining the appropriate savings compensation numbers.

First, let's look at the Cashwell's layaway plan based on the higher yield. Their savings compensation rate drops to only 3.7 percent or $306.67 per month in order for them to reach financial independence at age 67.

CASHWELL PRM LAYAWAY PLAN #2
CONTRIBUTION SCHEDULE

Fund plan for 30 years

Annual income of $100,000.00, increasing 2.34 percent per year

Beginning balance = $86,542.00

Contribute 3.68 percent of salary, invested weekly

Your employer will contribute 3 percent of salary

Annual interest rate = 8 percent, compounded daily

Year #	Beginning Balance	Ann. Contrib.	ER Contrib.	Earnings	End Balance
1.	86,542.00	3,680.00	3,000.00	7,476.10	100,698.10
2.	100,698.10	3,766.11	3,070.20	8,661.28	116,195.69

Year #	Beginning Balance	Ann. Contrib.	ER Contrib.	Earnings	End Balance
3.	116,195.69	3,854.24	3,142.04	9,958.33	133,150.30
4.	133,150.30	3,944.43	3,215.57	11,376.86	151,687.16
5.	151,687.16	4,036.73	3,290.81	12,927.31	171,942.01
6.	171,942.01	4,131.19	3,367.82	14,621.00	194,062.01
7.	194,062.01	4,227.86	3,446.62	16,470.17	218,206.66
8.	218,206.66	4,326.79	3,527.27	18,488.11	244,548.83
9.	244,548.83	4,428.04	3,609.81	20,689.22	273,275.90
10.	273,275.90	4,531.65	3,694.28	23,089.12	304,590.95
11.	304,590.95	4,637.69	3,780.73	25,704.72	338,714.08
12.	338,714.08	4,746.21	3,869.20	28,554.34	375,883.84
13.	375,883.84	4,857.28	3,959.74	31,657.87	416,358.72
14.	416,358.72	4,970.94	4,052.39	35,036.83	460,418.88
15.	460,418.88	5,087.26	4,147.22	38,714.56	508,367.92
16.	508,367.92	5,206.30	4,244.26	42,716.34	560,534.82
17.	560,534.82	5,328.13	4,343.58	47,069.59	617,276.12
18.	617,276.12	5,452.80	4,445.22	51,803.98	678,978.12
19.	678,978.12	5,580.40	4,549.24	56,951.70	746,059.46
20.	746,059.46	5,710.98	4,655.69	62,547.62	818,973.75
21.	818,973.75	5,844.62	4,764.63	68,629.52	898,212.52
22.	898,212.52	5,981.38	4,876.13	75,238.33	984,308.36
23.	984,308.36	6,121.35	4,990.23	82,418.42	1,077,838.36
24.	1,077,838.36	6,264.59	5,107.00	90,217.84	1,179,427.79

Year #	Beginning Balance	Ann. Contrib.	ER Contrib.	Earnings	End Balance
25.	1,179,427.79	6,411.18	5,226.50	98,688.68	1,289,754.15
26.	1,289,754.15	6,561.20	5,348.80	107,887.37	1,409,551.52
27.	1,409,551.52	6,714.73	5,473.96	117,875.03	1,539,615.24
28.	1,539,615.24	6,871.85	5,602.06	128,717.91	1,680,807.05
29.	1,680,807.05	7,032.66	5,733.14	140,487.78	1,834,060.63
30.	1,834,060.63	7,197.22	5,867.30	153,262.40	2,000,387.55
Totals		$157,505.81	$128,401.44	$1,627,938.33	

www.MyCalculators.com

Fortunately for the Freewheelers, there's still hope. In PRM Layaway Plan #2 we can see that their savings compensation rate will be easier to manage based on an assumed 8 percent rate of return.

In this scenario, they will need to have only $755 per month deducted from their salary to reach their goal.

FREEWHEELER LAYAWAY PLAN #2
CONTRIBUTION SCHEDULE

Fund plan for 30 years

Annual income of $ 100,000.00, increasing 2.34 percent per year

Beginning balance = $ 10,000.00

Contribute 9.061 percent of salary, invested weekly

Your employer will contribute 3 percent of salary, increasing 0 percent per year to a maximum of 3 percent, invested weekly

Annual interest rate = 8 percent, compounded daily

Year #	Beginning Balance	Ann. Contrib.	ER Contrib.	Earnings	End Balance
1.	10,000.00	9,061.00	3,000.00	1,318.63	23,379.63

Year #	Beginning Balance	Ann. Contrib.	ER Contrib.	Earnings	End Balance
2.	23,379.63	9,273.03	3,070.20	2,444.22	38,167.08
3.	38,167.08	9,490.02	3,142.04	3,687.32	54,486.46
4.	54,486.46	9,712.08	3,215.57	5,058.27	72,472.38
5.	72,472.38	9,939.35	3,290.81	6,568.28	92,270.81
6.	92,270.81	10,171.93	3,367.82	8,229.51	114,040.07
7.	114,040.07	10,409.95	3,446.62	10,055.17	137,951.80
8.	137,951.80	10,653.54	3,527.27	12,059.54	164,192.16
9.	164,192.16	10,902.83	3,609.81	14,258.14	192,962.95
10.	192,962.95	11,157.96	3,694.28	16,667.78	224,482.97
11.	224,482.97	11,419.06	3,780.73	19,306.69	258,989.45
12.	258,989.45	11,686.26	3,869.20	22,194.64	296,739.54
13.	296,739.54	11,959.72	3,959.74	25,353.03	338,012.03
14.	338,012.03	12,239.58	4,052.39	28,805.11	383,109.12
15.	383,109.12	12,525.99	4,147.22	32,576.05	432,358.37
16.	432,358.37	12,819.09	4,244.26	36,693.12	486,114.85
17.	486,114.85	13,119.06	4,343.58	41,185.92	544,763.41
18.	544,763.41	13,426.05	4,445.22	46,086.49	608,721.16
19.	608,721.16	13,740.22	4,549.24	51,429.58	678,440.19
20.	678,440.19	14,061.74	4,655.69	57,252.85	754,410.47
21.	754,410.47	14,390.78	4,764.63	63,597.11	837,163.00
22.	837,163.00	14,727.53	4,876.13	70,506.60	927,273.25
23.	927,273.25	15,072.15	4,990.23	78,029.24	1,025,364.87
24.	1,025,364.87	15,424.84	5,107.00	86,216.98	1,132,113.69

Year #	Beginning Balance	Ann. Contrib.	ER Contrib.	Earnings	End Balance
25.	1,132,113.69	15,785.78	5,226.50	95,126.12	1,248,252.09
26.	1,248,252.09	16,155.17	5,348.80	104,817.65	1,374,573.71
27.	1,374,573.71	16,533.20	5,473.96	115,357.68	1,511,938.56
28.	1,511,938.56	16,920.07	5,602.06	126,817.83	1,661,278.52
29.	1,661,278.52	17,316.00	5,733.14	139,275.73	1,823,603.40
30.	1,823,603.40	17,721.20	5,867.30	152,815.48	2,000,007.38
Totals		$387,815.18	$128,401.44	$1,473,790.76	

www.MyCalculators.com

As you can see, although the Freewheelers' savings compensation rate is lower based on an assumed 8 percent rate of return, they have to allocate a significantly higher percentage of their compensation as savings compensation than do the Cashwells. This is due entirely to the fact that the Cashwells made the commitment to start saving early and stayed away from excess spending. They understood that part of their salary was savings compensation and that only the remainder was available for spending.

For the Freewheelers, the cost of waiting to start saving properly will in essence be nearly 5 percent of their income for the rest of their working life! In spite of this situation, the Freewheelers still have the opportunity to build wealth and acquire their PRM. If they can earn an 8 percent rate of return and their employer contributes a 3 percent matching contribution to their 401(k), they would need to divert only 9.06 percent of their salary as savings compensation. I have calculated that between age 27 and 37, the Cashwells put $31,840 more into their 401(k) than the Freewheelers did during that same time.

Given their current savings level, the Freewheelers will need to contribute $205,870 more than the Cashwells over the next 30 years to arrive at the same $2,000,000 goal. Looking at this another way, if the Freewheelers saved the same amount as the Cashwells from this point forward, assuming a 7 percent annual rate of return, they would amass only $1,313,328 over the next 30 years compared to the Cashwells' $2 million.

In other words, by starting to save early, the Cashwells turned $31,840 into nearly $687,000 in additional assets at age 67. Wow!

My guess is that many of my readers in their mid to late 40s are a bit concerned, if not frustrated, in trying to figure out how they can build their own PRM. You're not alone if you believe that you should have started saving earlier or saved more when you were younger. In fact, you are more like the norm. You can see that time is your greatest ally, but you now have less of it than you would like. You're concerned that your savings compensation percentage will simply be too high for you to be able to pay your bills. Please don't despair, there are methods to accomplish your goals and allow you to enjoy your lifestyle today. The bottom line is that you need a game changer. Let's say, for example, you are 45 and your financial plans of the past are more like the Freewheelers than the Cashwells, but you are ready to put together a plan and commit yourself to accomplishing this valuable goal. You are willing to acknowledge that this is a challenge you will need to face head-on without wavering once you begin.

We will need to create a PRM that is less expensive to acquire, given you have fewer years in your layaway plan to accumulate the necessary funds. Think of your PRM as if it were an engine that produces a stream of income. The more income it needs to produce, the more fuel (investment dollars) you need to put into it. Thus, if we can design your PRM in a way that makes it easier to produce income throughout your financial freedom years, we can reduce the amount of fuel required to make the engine run as long as you need it to. Two numbers we can change to allow your PRM engine to run with less fuel are the *inflation rate of your income stream* from the PRM and the *percentage reduction of income* at the beginning of the subsequent thirds of your financial freedom years. Both of these options are relatively reasonable given the most common spending habits and/or financial needs of people as they age.

The real game changer is your desired age for financial freedom. Moving that back one year to age 68, for example, can make a substantial difference. This can also be accomplished by working part time or working in a different, more enjoyable profession for a year or two after you leave your career job. This would give you an additional year of contributions and earnings accumulation in your PRM layaway plan and reduce the number of years your PRM would be expected to provide income. So let's look at a PRM model that's designed for easier entry, given you have fewer years to fund your layaway plan.

I'm going to call you the "Late Bloomers."

For you, I'm going to create a financial model using the following assumptions:

- You're age 45 and have saved a total of $68,000 to date.

- You are willing to work an extra year and plan to declare financial freedom at age 68.

- You currently earn $100,000 per year, and your income will increase by 2.34 percent per year; thus your pre-freedom income will be $166,340, and your PRM will need to produce approximately $83,170 per year for you to begin financial freedom.

We will assume a 7.5 percent rate of return during your accumulation years and review differing rates of return in your PRM during your financial independence. Your savings compensation will need to be 10.7 percent of your gross salary.

LATE BLOOMER PRM LAYAWAY PLAN CONTRIBUTION SCHEDULE

Fund plan for 23 years

Annual income of $ 100,000.00, increasing 2.34 percent per year

Beginning balance = $ 68,000.00

Contribute 10.7 percent of salary, invested monthly

Your employer will contribute 3 percent of salary, invested annually

Annual interest rate = 7.5 percent, compounded annually

Year #	Beginning Balance	Ann. Contrib.	ER Contrib.	Earnings	End Balance
1.	68,000.00	10,700.00	3,000.00	5,463.01	87,163.01
2.	87,163.01	10,950.38	3,070.20	6,908.73	108,092.32
3.	108,092.32	11,206.62	3,142.04	8,487.12	130,928.10
4.	130,928.10	11,468.85	3,215.57	10,208.70	155,821.23
5.	155,821.23	11,737.22	3,290.81	12,084.79	182,934.05
6.	182,934.05	12,011.88	3,367.82	14,127.57	212,441.32
7.	212,441.32	12,292.95	3,446.62	16,350.15	244,531.04
8.	244,531.04	12,580.61	3,527.27	18,766.64	279,405.57
9.	279,405.57	12,875.00	3,609.81	21,392.22	317,282.59
10.	317,282.59	13,176.27	3,694.28	24,243.21	358,396.36

Year #	Beginning Balance	Ann. Contrib.	ER Contrib.	Earnings	End Balance
11.	358,396.36	13,484.59	3,780.73	27,337.21	402,998.89
12.	402,998.89	13,800.13	3,869.20	30,693.10	451,361.32
13.	451,361.32	14,123.06	3,959.74	34,331.24	503,775.35
14.	503,775.35	14,453.54	4,052.39	38,273.50	560,554.79
15.	560,554.79	14,791.75	4,147.22	42,543.44	622,037.19
16.	622,037.19	15,137.88	4,244.26	47,166.36	688,585.70
17.	688,585.70	15,492.10	4,343.58	52,169.51	760,590.89
18.	760,590.89	15,854.62	4,445.22	57,582.20	838,472.94
19.	838,472.94	16,225.62	4,549.24	63,435.94	922,683.73
20.	922,683.73	16,605.30	4,655.69	69,764.63	1,013,709.35
21.	1,013,709.35	16,993.86	4,764.63	76,604.74	1,112,072.59
22.	1,112,072.59	17,391.52	4,876.13	83,995.47	1,218,335.70
23.	1,218,335.70	17,798.48	4,990.23	91,979.01	1,333,103.42
Totals		**$321,152.23**	**$90,042.68**	**$853,908.49**	

For the Late Bloomers, it's not too late to create a solid plan for financial success. In this example, we see that only a 10.7 percent savings rate was required to take $68,000 and turn it into a PRM valued at $1,333,103, assuming an average annual rate of return of 7.5 percent, which is not guaranteed. We now need to design a PRM that will produce income for at least 27 years and have a reasonable reliability of success.

In this projection for financial freedom, we illustrate how your PRM will provide a 2 percent increase in income each year to offset inflation. In anticipation of reduced financial needs at older ages, it will reduce your income (based on initial freedom income amount) at each third of your 27 years of financial freedom. It will reduce income by 12 percent at age 77 and by 18 percent at age 87. As you will see in the Late Bloomer Distribution Schedule, the actual income at age 77 is greater than the initial income amount, and the income at age 87 is similar to that of age 77. The point here is that in spite of these income reductions based on changes in spending habits, the actual amount of income provided by the PRM never goes below the age 77 inflation-adjusted level. The distribution schedule below will illustrate how the Late Bloomer's PRM will produce income for 28 years and then have a remaining balance of $132,786.

The table below assumes a rate of return of 6 percent on your PRM assets. If you're concerned about your ability to achieve a 6 percent rate of return, we have also calculated that with just a 5.7 percent rate of return, the Late Bloomer's PRM would provide income for the 28 years needed. Returns used in these examples are assumptions only. They are not guaranteed, nor do they represent any particular investment. However, at the lower rate of return there would not be a remaining balance.

LATE BLOOMER DISTRIBUTION SCHEDULE

Spend 27 years in retirement

Amount saved at time of retirement = $ 1,333,103

Annual interest rate = 6 percent (compounded annually)

Annual inflation rate = 2 percent

$132,786 remaining in the account at age 95/96

Age	Beginning Balance	Withdrawals	Earnings	Portfolio Balance
68	$ 1,333,103	$ 83,172	$ 74,996	$1,324,927

Age	Beginning Balance	Withdrawals	Earnings	Portfolio Balance
69	$ 1,324,927	$84,835	$74,405	$1,314,497
70	$ 1,313,497	$86,532	$73,678	$1,301,643
71	$ 1,301,643	$88,263	$72,803	$1,286,183
72	$ 1,286,183	$90,028	$71,769	$1,267,924
73	$ 1,267,924	$91,829	$70,566	$1,246,661
74	$ 1,246,661	$93,665	$69,180	$1,222,176
75	$ 1,222,176	$95,538	$67,598	$1,194,235
76	$ 1,194,235	$97,449	$65,807	$1,162,593
77	$ 1,162,593	$87,466	$64,508	$1,139,634
78	$1,139,634	$89,216	$63,025	$1,113,444
79	$ 1,113,444	$91,000	$61,347	$1,083,790
80	$ 1,083,790	$92,820	$59,458	$1,050,428
81	$ 1,050,428	$94,676	$57,345	$1,013,097
82	$ 1,013,097	$96,570	$54,992	$971,519
83	$ 971,519	$98,501	$52,381	$925,398
84	$ 925,398	$100,471	$49,496	$874,422
85	$ 874,422	$102,481	$46,316	$818,258
86	$ 818,258	$104,530	$42,824	$756,551
87	$ 756,551	$87,426	$40,148	$709,273
88	$ 709,273	$89,175	$37,206	$657,304
89	$ 657,304	$90,958	$33,981	$600,326
90	$ 600,326	$92,777	$30,453	$538,002
91	$ 538,002	$94,633	$26,602	$469,971

Age	Beginning Balance	Withdrawals	Earnings	Portfolio Balance
92	$ 469,971	$96,526	$22,407	$395,852
93	$ 395,852	$98,456	$17,844	$315,240
94	$ 315,240	$100,425	$12,889	$227,704
95	$ 227,704	$102,434	$7,516	$132,786
TOTAL INCOME			**$2,621,852**	

Remember, *it's never too late to start building wealth.* A key to building wealth is your commitment to achieving success and consistency in your savings habits. Another important consideration is your investment strategy. A well-designed portfolio will give you your best chance of success in achieving the returns we have assumed.

In looking at all of the various scenarios we've projected, another valuable takeaway from the information illustrated is *the power of 1 percent* in additional returns in your portfolio. This is also an important consideration for those people who may invest too conservatively because they are simply unsure about how to invest wisely. Continuously investing in ultraconservative investments can rob you of an opportunity to realize your dreams of financial independence and diminish the value of your savings based on the effects of inflation. Consider that if the Cashwells contributed the same amount as established in Layaway Plan #1 ($297,891 over 30 years) but earned an 8 percent rate of return instead of 7 percent, they would have accumulated an additional $325,000! You can also see that the increased returns from that additional 1 percent are greater for the Cashwells, who have a significantly larger initial account balance, than for the Freewheelers.

I'm sure you've heard the old saying "You've got to have money to make money."

Earning that extra 1 percent can come from having a well-thought-out investment strategy and sticking with it. A properly balanced portfolio can help manage risk and take advantage of a broad scope of opportunities in different investment sectors. Proper diversification is particularly important when markets are volatile, as it may help you avoid the full impact of sharp market declines. An increased return can also come in part by avoiding excess fees on your investments. I have reviewed 401(k) plans where the fees being charged were as much as 1 percent more than the fees of more competitive plans.

With the advent of recent ERISA legislation requiring fee disclosure, these problems are being addressed around the country. Imagine that just seeking the right advice from a qualified advisor and being careful not to pay excess fees could potentially add hundreds of thousands of dollars to your savings or enable you to achieve financial independence with 2 to 3 percent lower salary deductions required over your working life.

The message here is quite simple, albeit difficult for some of us to accept. The ability for you to one day declare financial independence requires savings discipline, a well-designed investment strategy, and a degree of sacrifice. When you consider the benefits of true financial freedom, it isn't hard to understand why something so great would be well worth such an effort.

Achieving financial freedom requires starting *as early as possible* and also knowing that *it's never too late to create a plan for your future.* To have a successful savings discipline requires you to be *consistent* with your layaway plan and to *keep your goal in sight*, especially when you're tempted to buy something that you really can't afford. Remember that part of your salary is savings compensation and that *spending compensation* is what's left over after that. Be careful to know the difference between *good debt* and *bad debt* and stay away from creating bad debt. Good debt is using debt to buy necessities like your residence, a car (within your means), and things to help increase your income such as education, a computer, or investments in your own business. Bad debt is from using credit to buy non-necessity items that you can't pay for in cash. These are often things like toys, vacations, or expensive cars that are more luxurious than necessary.

The interest on bad debt is the annual penalty for buying something you couldn't really afford. That penalty reduces your disposable income and thus reduces the amount you would have available to fund your layaway plan, ultimately to buy your PRM.

ACTION ITEMS

If you haven't already established your goals for financial freedom, do that immediately. You will need to determine the age at which you plan to declare financial independence before you can calculate the cost of your PRM.

Seek the assistance of a financial advisor or use a financial calculator to determine the percentage of your salary required to be savings compensation, considering what you currently have saved and a reasonable projection of your rate of return.

Contact your financial advisor, and review your current debt to determine the best ways to reduce interest costs and pay off excesses. Debt consolidation to low-rate programs and/or home equity credit lines can be an effective method of lowering debt service costs that may be eating away at your disposable income.

Adjust your 401(k) plan contributions according to the appropriate savings compensation percentage.

Begin to evaluate your portfolio allocation to determine if it is properly balanced. See later chapters for more information.

CHAPTER 7

INVESTMENT ALLOCATION TECHNIQUES

"If you want to always have some investments in the top-performing market sectors, you should allocate your money to all of them." —Richard Cella

When I first entered the business of 401(k) plans in 1988, I was taught that it was all about

- dollar cost averaging;

- time in the market, not market timing; and

- diversification through mutual funds.

These were the "big three" steps to a successful investment strategy. Back in the late 1980s this made sense. No one had ever heard of an exchange traded fund (ETF). The general word was that unless you had substantial wealth, individual stock investing was too risky, and commodity investing was only for people who understood the changing demand for pork bellies and the effect of the weather on the orange crop. Some of the first 401(k) plans I saw implemented had only four mutual fund investment choices! This uninspiring array would include a stock fund, a foreign stock fund, a bond fund, and a money market fund.

As the stock market grew in the 1990s, interest in 401(k) plans exploded and so did the array of specialized mutual funds. Mutual fund companies and third party 401(k) vendors began offering 401(k) plans with a broader, more creative array of investment choices. It became desirable to have fund managers that focused on smaller companies, technology companies, midsized companies poised for growth, large growth companies, and on and on. Initially, this worked quite well, and all the theories of diversification through mutual funds, dollar cost averaging, and just spending time in the market for the long haul made perfect sense. People got more and more aggressive by investing in mid cap and small cap funds, Internet funds, and technology funds. The stock market was raging forward like a bull, and it looked as though nothing could stop it. Then came the "technology bubble" in 2001 and the first in a series of the stock market crashes that began wiping out 401(k) accounts while simultaneously changing the way people must look at their 401(k) investment strategy.

The ways of the 1980s and 1990s just weren't working anymore. Even I was wondering how these tried-and-true methods were failing. Then it became clear. When the stock market is rallying like a raging bull, it's easy to hide inefficiencies in strategy and high expenses. When a monkey can throw darts at the stock page of a newspaper and select good, profitable investments, anyone with a little talent can justify their existence. Today, I think it's clear that we may not see the type of bull market seen in the 1990s for a long while, if ever. With economic challenges, high government debt, and a fragile global economy, we may experience a sideways moving and/or volatile stock market for many years to come. Therefore, we need a new strategy that includes more choices, lower fees, and more advanced concepts for managing money to take advantage of economic trends.

Today, many 401(k) plan advisors would suggest that their ideal investment selection would offer some 30-plus investment choices, including mutual funds, ETFs, alternative investments such as real estate or commodity funds, and "target retirement date" managed portfolios. In addition, plan sponsors may consider offering an outside brokerage account option where participants can choose to invest in everything from individual stocks to options trading. We believe that choice is *critical* as long as participants have the knowledge to make the right choices. I also believe that it is a 401(k) plan participant's right to have the opportunity to choose from the complete array of investment styles in the universe of investment options available today. Plan participants should have the opportunity to determine their optimal portfolio based on their own personal circumstances and current economic conditions. Most important to note is that the old standard way of dollar cost averaging into three or four mutual funds and sitting pat with the same asset allocation may simply be your best option.

Let's debunk the myth.

Let's take the "big three" steps to a successful investment strategy and break them down.

DOLLAR COST AVERAGING (DCA)

I have often given the example of "The Tale of Two Investors" and advised people that dollar cost averaging was one of most effective ways to offset a poor market and prepare to profit from the recovery. You may also recall that, in chapter 5, I made DCA one of the Seven Rules for Successful Investing. Of course, I still believe this to be true. The question now is: *how can you effectively use this tool in your 401(k) plan?*

I would give the example of two investors, Bill and Mary, who each invested the same $200 per month into a stock over a period of two years. At the outset of their investment strategy, both stocks were priced at the same $10 per share, but Bill's stock kept going up consistently month after month to a peak of $20 at the end of the two years. Mary's stock didn't do so well. It started going down gradually from $10 all the way to $5, and then after the midpoint of the two years began climbing gradually back to $10, where it ended. In fact, Mary's stock never went over the original $10 price during the two years. So which investor made more money? If you say Bill (the guy now holding stock valued at $20), you're wrong. It's Mary!

As you will see in the chart, although Bill ("Investor A") picked a great stock that went up from $10 per share to $20 per share over the two-year period, the fact that he was dollar cost averaging meant that as share prices went up he was buying fewer shares at higher prices. On the other hand, as Mary's ("Investor B") stock was going down in price she was buying more shares at low prices, so when the stock came back to its original price she had purchased many shares at lower prices that yielded strong profits. You've heard the old adage "Buy low, sell high"? The result is that Mary turned in a profit of $1,550.50 while Bill made only $1,191.20.

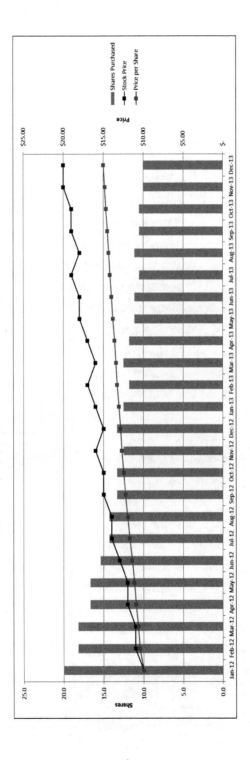

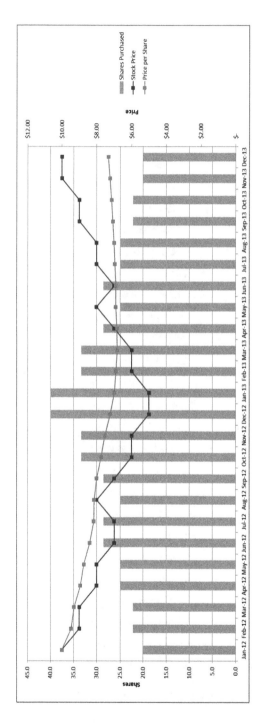

Investment Comparison		
	Investor A	Investor B
Total Investment	$ 4,800	$ 4,800
Opening Stock Price	$ 10	$ 10
Closing Stock Price	$ 20	$ 10
Total Shares Owned	320	655
Average Price Paid	$ 15.02	$ 7.33
Profit/Loss	$ 1,591.89	$ 1,750.79

The principal behind dollar cost averaging is that when stock prices are high you buy fewer shares and when prices go down you buy more shares at lower prices. This assures you of having an efficient cost basis for your investments over the long run as well as remaining positioned to take advantage of price rebounds after a decline. However, there is one problem: you can't be sure to get this benefit from mutual funds.

To say this differently, investing a like amount of money into a mutual fund at regular intervals over a period of years *is not* necessarily dollar cost averaging. Investing a like amount of money at regular intervals into the same *stock* or the same index of stocks over a number of years *is* dollar cost averaging.

The reason you cannot effectively establish DCA with most mutual funds is that the mutual fund managers trade stocks within their portfolio all the time (unless it's an index fund). A year from now it won't be unreasonable to presume that the holdings in the ABC mutual fund will be completely different from what they were when you started investing. Therefore, the benefit of buying low may not hold true and is assuredly diluted by the frequent trading within the mutual fund.

In addition, as other shareholders sell their mutual fund shares, the fund manager may sell some of the shares of the stock you bought low to pay them out. Or, as other people invest new dollars into the mutual fund, the manager may decide to buy a heavy weighting in a new stock that has already appreciated in price because he or she wants to dress up the portfolio with a top-performing stock. As a shareholder in that fund, your holdings include a share of all of these transactions.

In short, you have no control over which stocks are held in a mutual fund portfolio or when they're bought and sold. The only type of fund that you may successfully retain the full effect of DCA is an index fund such as an exchange traded fund (ETF). Because these funds invest in a pre-established index of stocks or bonds such as the S&P 500, the composition of the fund does not change in terms of holdings as investors buy or sell. Thus, you can be assured that the stock you bought when the market was down is the stock you'll own when the market goes back up.

ACTION STRATEGY

Review your current 401(k) plan investments and the list of offerings made available to you. Attempt to identify which funds are index funds or exchange traded funds. Seek to incorporate two or more index funds into your asset allocation.

If your plan does not offer index funds or exchange traded funds, make a request to your HR department to investigate such options. The first place to start would be an S&P 500 Index fund/ETF, S&P Mid Cap 400 Index fund, and Russell 2000 Index fund. This covers the large cap, mid cap, and small cap domestic stock sectors that you can use for dollar cost averaging.

"SPEND TIME IN THE MARKET ..."

The second of the "big three" is spending "time in the market, not timing the market." Simply put, being *patient*. The attempt to buy or sell based on a presumption of market movements carries the risk of missing the market that is a substantially higher risk than simply investing in the stock market. If you were to do this repeatedly and guess wrong, you could suffer losses and/or significantly underperform the general investment markets. I personally believe that market timing is a dangerous game for the average investor. This is because of a number of basic truths. One of these truths is most people allow emotion as opposed to facts and knowledge to be their guide. That's a recipe for poor investment results.

Another basic truth is that most people are not really educated enough to know when to proactively make timing trades in their portfolios. Most people would sell because stocks have gone down and buy after stocks have gone up. Even for those astute investors who have the knowledge, they often don't have the time to pay enough attention to make changes at the right time.

On the other hand, if you decide to stand pat no matter what goes on in the economy or the world around you, it feels like lying down to let the traders on Wall Street pick your pockets.

Regardless of how it feels to watch your portfolio lose value in down markets, the simple fact is that most investors do not earn returns consistent with the stock market in spite of putting their money into the market and bearing the risks associated with such investments. The table below shows the average returns of stock market and balanced investors over various time periods versus the performance of the S&P 500 Index (widely considered representative of the US stock market).

AVERAGE ANNUAL RETURNS
1991 THROUGH 2010

	INVESTOR RETURNS				
	Equity Fund Investors	Asset Alloc. Funds	Investor Composite	Inflation	S&P 500
30 Year	3.79	1.76	2.47	2.7	11.06
20 Year	5.19	2.47	3.34	2.28	9.85
10 Year	5.26	2.25	3.51	2.13	7.67
5 Year	10.19	5.09	6.84	1.69	15.45
3 Year	14.82	7.15	9.57	1.39	20.41
12 Mo's.	5.5	2.24	3.98	0.75	13.69

1. Source: DALBAR, Inc., Quantitative Analysis of Investor Behavior, 2015 (QAIB 2015). "QAIB 2015" examines real investor returns in equity, fixed income, and asset allocation funds as well as the composite returns for these investors. The analysis shows the average annual returns for investors covering the 30-year period ended December 31, 2014. The S&P 500 Index is a broad-based measure of domestic stock market performance that includes the reinvestment of dividends. The index is unmanaged and cannot be purchased directly by investors. Index performance and the DALBAR study results are shown for illustrative purposes only and does not predict or depict the performance of any investment. Past performance does not guarantee future results.

Past performance does not guarantee future results. Due to ongoing market volatility, current performance may be more or less than the results shown in this presentation. The performance information does not show the effects of income taxes on an individual's investment. Taxes may reduce your actual investment returns or any gains you may realize if you sell your investment. An investor's shares, when redeemed, may be worth more or less than the original cost.

Why do investors fair so poorly in comparison to the general stock market? The answer is simple. Investors tend to "chase returns" and in doing so, they continuously sell certain investments at low points in favor of buying other investments that are reaching high points. This process of chasing returns is akin to a puppy chasing its own tail: you don't have much chance of catching up to the returns you saw previously reported. Conversely, a dollar cost averaging investor would continue to buy into a diversified set of investment sectors, buying more shares when prices are low and fewer shares when prices are high. Which method would you prefer? It is undoubtedly a challenge to be a successful investor in that we must balance knowledge and discipline against the emotional desire to chase after what appear to be better performing investments.

When given the advice that you will need to invest money into a portfolio for the long term, you may question how to do that so that you weather the storms that the markets can throw at you over time. It's easy to say that investors should simply spend a long period of time in the market. However, when your account values are declining and you see those statements with negative returns, it's hard to find the confidence to stick with your investment allocation.

The first thing that you need is the knowledge that your investments are properly allocated. If you aren't sure of that, you should make that a priority. This helps you avoid emotional distress when one or more of your investment funds are not doing well. It also helps you control the impulse to chase last years' top performers— the impulse to *chase returns*.

The next thing an investor needs is a set of guidelines that outline what type of trading and how much would be advisable in given circumstances.

Let's establish some basic rules for making adjustments to your portfolio. I think it would be unwise to make wholesale changes to an asset allocation that was properly established at the outset. In other words, if you do your homework, determine your risk tolerance, and establish the appropriate asset allocation, portfolio management should be limited to minor periodic adjustments to your portfolio. There will not be a need to make dramatic changes as markets change but only when your risk tolerance changes for reasons such as age or proximity to financial freedom.

There are several circumstances under which modifications to your asset allocation would be warranted. *The first step in portfolio management, once you establish the right asset allocation, is to rebalance your portfolio annually.* This means that if you started out with 75 percent of your assets in stock and 25 percent in bonds, at the end of the year you should transfer funds from those areas that grew the most to those that didn't. This way you will reestablish the same 75/25 mix to start the next year. This will help sell some of your investments reaching new heights and buy into other sectors while they're low. This will also help maintain the appropriate levels of risk and diversification in your portfolio.

The second scenario that may give rise to changing your asset allocation mix would be adverse economic conditions such as a recession or depression. However, this is where portfolio management becomes more complex. You must first understand the fundamentals of proper diversification before you can proceed. Dollar cost averaging, asset allocation, and rebalancing are the tools that should enable you to have the confidence to spend time in the market and avoid market timing.

DIVERSIFICATION AND PORTFOLIO MANAGEMENT

In 1952 Harry Markowitz created "modern portfolio theory," using complex mathematical equations that determined the risk levels of a diversified portfolio versus a portfolio of a singular type of investment such as 100 percent stock. These equations seemed to justify the theory that an investor could lower risk and still garner a similar long-term return by investing in a diverse portfolio of stock market sectors mixed with bonds and cash. I have established diversification as one of my Seven Rules for Successful Investing. Unfortunately, many people believe they are diversified when in fact they're not. With that in mind, let's take a look at diversification and what it really means.

I've always said that *if you want a portfolio that will always have investments in the top-performing market sectors, you should allocate investments to all of them*—the idea being that when you spread your investments over the entire spectrum of investment sectors, you will always have some of your money performing at the top. This would bode well for an investor in bear markets because they would have money invested elsewhere such as bonds, commodities, or foreign securities that may be doing well while our stock market isn't. This type of diversification is also referred to as *asset allocation strategy*.

In today's investment world, diversification means something very different than it did 20 years ago. The investment markets have expanded, and the variety of market sectors available to the average investor has also expanded. The biggest factor affecting the landscape of asset allocation is that we are now in a truly global economy. The health of international economies has never had a more profound effect on the US economy, commodity prices, interest rates, bond values, and stock prices. A survey of five of the largest publicly traded corporations in the United States (Google, Microsoft, GE, Pfizer, and Merck) found that as of 2008, they derived more than 50 percent of their revenues on average from foreign markets.[3]

Thus, if economic shifts take place in foreign countries, these changes will have an effect on the health of our economy and/or our stock markets.

One of the reasons we recommend a number of specialized ETFs for our retirement plans is that with ETFs you can invest directly into well-defined investment strategies, such as real estate, commodities, and natural resources. These funds enable you to invest in these markets through an index of stocks of companies in a specific industry sector. By having funds that clearly identify the sector they focus investments on, we can position them in the appropriate percentage to both diversify and manage our portfolios. When designing a portfolio, we can also diversify through funds that have narrowly defined strategies in a specific stock sector, such as dividend paying stocks, industry sectors such as health care, or specific geographic regions such as the emerging foreign markets.

There are two general types of diversification when it comes to the investment portfolio styles: fundamental asset allocation and tactical asset allocation. Modern portfolio theory is synonymous with *fundamental asset allocation,* whereby portfolios are created based on a stagnant allocation of stocks, bonds, commodities, and so on, according to risk tolerance levels. *Tactical asset allocation* starts out similarly but with the intent that there will be dynamic adjustments to the allocations as economic circumstances change or possibly as other circumstances change such as the age of the investor.

---

3 Goldman Sachs Global Markets Institute survey of company reports.

Fortunately, many 401(k) plans offer various types of diversified portfolios such as "lifestyle funds" or "target retirement date funds." *Lifestyle funds* are pre-established asset allocation models that participants can choose based on their risk tolerance such as aggressive, moderate, or conservative. This is a fundamental asset allocation where a mix of stock and bond funds is blended together in differing percentages based on the risk level intended for each portfolio. *Target retirement date funds* are fundamental asset allocation models with an element of dynamic asset management. This type of investment will be managed to adjust the allocations automatically as you get closer to declaring your financial freedom, the *target date,* by reducing exposure to risk investments in favor of heavier weightings in more conservative investments like bonds and money markets. This is based on the theory that as you get closer to declaring your financial freedom, you will have a lower tolerance for risk. You select these funds by the date in the name such as the "Target Date 2025 fund." This would indicate that you plan to declare financial freedom in the year 2025 or close to it. Target date funds are attractive for investors who are over age 50 and who are unsure about how and/or when to reallocate their investments to account for changes in risk tolerance. They are also very convenient in that the adjustments to the portfolio are made automatically as you approach financial independence.

In order to have an understanding of the various degrees of diversification, let's first get a basic understanding of fundamental asset allocation. With this method, we allocate the heaviest weighting of stock investments to the aggressive portfolio and reduce equity (stock) exposure for each level of lower risk such as moderate or conservative. Here are several examples of fundamental asset allocation models based on risk tolerance.

Aggressive Portfolio

Peer Group	Total
Large Cap Growth	14%
Large Cap Value	10%
Large Cap Blend	6%
Mid Cap Growth	16%
Foreign Large Cap	10%
Small Cap Growth	12%
Int'l Small Mid Cap	6%
Emerging Markets	10%
Real Estate	6%
Intermediate Bond	5%
Stable Value/Money	5%
	100.00%

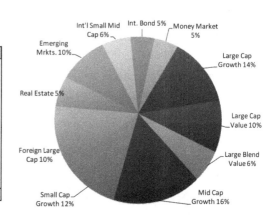

Moderate Portfolio

Peer Group	Total
Large Cap Growth	10%
Large Cap Value	17%
Int'l Large Value	10%
Mid Cap Blend	10%
Small Cap Growth	6%
Real Estate	7%
Intermediate Bond	20%
Inflation Protected Bond	6%
Multi Sector Bond	6%
Stable Value/Money Market	8%
	100.00%

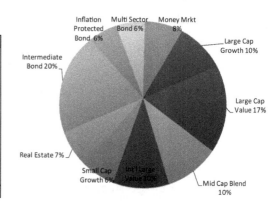

Conservative Portfolio

Peer Group	Total
Large Cap Value	10%
Large Blend	10%
Mid Cap Value	10%
Intermediate Bond	20%
Inflation Protected Bond	20%
Multi Sector Bond	10%
Global Bond	5%
Stable Value/Money Market	15%
	100.00%

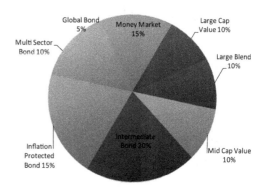

As you can see in the aggressive portfolio, 84 percent of the funds in the portfolio are stock funds, and 6 percent is devoted to stocks of real estate companies, for a total of 90 percent stock. In the moderate portfolio, we incorporate only 60 percent stock funds into the mix, with the balance going into bond and money market funds. In the conservative portfolio, there is only 30 percent allocated to stock. You might also imagine that we can create several different portfolio styles in between these risk levels, such as *moderately aggressive* with 75 percent stock, *balanced* with 50 percent stock, *moderately conservative* with 40 percent stock, and *ultraconservative* with no stock.

A well-diversified asset allocation model will hold as many as 12 to 14 different holdings, depending on market conditions. These portfolios are truly diversified to include investments in the small, medium, and large cap stock sectors, international markets, commodities, real estate, and various bond investment styles and cash equivalents. I advise my clients that *to be truly diversified your portfolio must also hold investments that are not directly correlated to stock market performance such as real estate and commodities.*

I believe that investment allocations to commodities and natural resources such as agricultural products and energy will reduce the risk factors in a portfolio over time. This belief is based on the premise that these investments are made in the appropriate amounts given the various economic conditions. Generally speaking, a 3–10 percent allocation to a basket of the various commodities is appropriate for a moderate to aggressive investor.

When the economy is in an above average inflationary trend, commodities will perform very well. When inflation is held in check and the US dollar is stronger than world currencies, commodities can underperform.

The advantages of a properly diversified portfolio such as those shown previously can be significant. First, by selecting a portfolio that is based on your true risk tolerance (don't cheat!), you can establish a reasonable understanding of the potential range of volatility in portfolio values that can be expected over the long term. If the right portfolio style is chosen, this potential volatility in any given market would be consistent with what you are comfortable with. Diversification by nature will help you smooth out the volatility of different investment markets and may help establish a degree of downside protection from bear markets. However, that does not guarantee that your investments won't lose value in a down market.

Most importantly, you can take confidence that your money is invested in an efficient manner given your personal objectives and will provide reasonable returns consistent with your asset allocation style over the long term. This confidence is critical. *One of the most potentially damaging things an investor can do to his or her portfolio is to attempt to time the market based on emotional reactions.* The odds are that the average investor will guess wrong most of the time. Even if you're smart enough to sell out of the market in time to avoid a downturn, when will you reinvest back into the market? The real answer to that question is usually ... after it goes back up. As a result, market timing increases risk and generally reduces returns.

The key to best using fundamental asset allocation to your advantage is to keep your emotions in check and have confidence that the portfolio will grow over time even when markets are doing poorly. This is easier said than done. Some financial gurus criticize fundamental asset allocation for being stagnant. They claim this stagnation in a portfolio leaves it subject to risk during adverse markets. While there may be some truth to that, it's far better having your money in a stagnant, well-diversified portfolio through a bear market than it is to have an improperly weighted portfolio and get slammed much harder.

One way to use this criticism to your advantage is to understand how tactical adjustments to your portfolio can reduce the effects of adverse market conditions and also reduce the chances of making a big mistake with your money. However, making tactical adjustments requires a good understanding of differing economic conditions, and the effects those conditions have on the investment markets. You must also have the discipline to stay within the guidelines of tactical management. You may need to consult a financial advisor for this type of guidance. Keep in mind that diversification is your friend during volatile markets. In order to be in a position to make the right tactical adjustments, you must first be in the right fundamental asset allocation model.

ACTION ITEMS

Take the time to complete a "risk assessment questionnaire" to determine your ideal risk tolerance. Most 401(k) plan vendors offer access to such questionnaires on their website or as part of your enrollment materials for the plan. Keep in mind that there are no wrong answers to these questions; it's most important that you answer the questions honestly based on your personal feelings and not the thoughts or beliefs of anyone else.

With the understanding of your ideal risk tolerance level, select an appropriate asset allocation model. Most 401(k) plans offer pre-established asset allocation models or lifestyle funds with titles based on a risk classification. Con-

*sider those professionally designed models as a guide
for your portfolio, or select the model that most closely
reflects your risk profile as your 401(k) plan investment.
If your plan does not offer any asset allocation models,
seek the advice of a financial advisor.*

UNDERSTANDING YOUR INVESTMENTS

Before I can speak about the types of circumstances that should trigger portfolio adjustments, let me first render some basic explanation of the type of securities you might be investing in within your 401(k). As I've pointed out, your investment choices will most likely be various mutual funds and ETFs. These funds will be stock, foreign stock, commodity, real estate, bond, and cash equivalent funds. There will be variations of the types of stock and the types of bonds these funds will be investing in, and those variations will have an important meaning in designing your portfolio.

STOCKS

Owning common stock in a corporation indicates that you have an ownership stake in that company. If ABC Co. has 1 million shares outstanding and you own 100 shares, you own .01 percent of that company. Owning stock gives you the right to vote on company policies and receive a share of the corporate profits should there be a dividend declared. The hope is that your company grows by increases in revenues and profits over time. This will make owning the company attractive to other investors and may result in them bidding up the stock price to reflect that growing value. For many people, it's too risky to invest a lot of money in one particular company, and it may be difficult to keep up on all the financial news of that company. This is why many people invest in stock mutual funds that are professionally managed and diversified among many different stocks.

Stocks are distinguished based on the size of the company in terms of market capitalization (the total value of their stock) and whether they represent a "value stock" or a "growth stock." A *value stock* is a company whose stock price is somewhat below the projected value based on other companies like it on the market, whereas a *growth stock* is a company whose stock is priced above current value based on the presumption of accelerated growth in the near term. Another general distinction of stock types is stocks of larger companies that pay dividends are often considered large cap value stocks whereas stocks of larger companies that don't pay dividends are considered large cap growth stocks. Typically, a value stock has a relatively high level of current earnings per share, a strong history of profits, dividend distributions, and/or an established leadership position in their industry. A growth stock will commonly have fast-growing revenues, profits and leading edge products or technologies, and is growing market share in their industry.

Stocks of smaller companies and midsize companies are more growth oriented by nature. Those small cap and mid cap companies that have exceptionally strong earnings and balance sheets are referred to as value stocks. Those companies with fast growing revenues that are expanding in size and scope may be considered growth stocks. Stocks of companies that may have new technologies or innovative products that might indicate expanding trends in our society are often considered growth stocks. Growth stocks are priced based on the perception of their future sales growth and near-term earnings growth and the potential for their products to have increased market share. As a result, growth stocks can be more volatile if their sales and earnings reports are disappointing to investors. They also have the potential for explosive growth if their products do well in the marketplace.

The table below is referred to as a "style box." There are essentially nine styles of stocks, which are duplicated for foreign stocks. For example, there is domestic large cap value and foreign large cap value. There's also a middle ground between value and growth, called "blend." This is helpful in describing mutual funds and ETFs that may include a mix of growth and value stocks as well as stocks that offer a blend of the characteristics described above.

	Value	Blend	Growth
Large Cap	18%	20%	26%
Mid Cap	6	8	10
Small Cap	3	3	6

The table above is an example of the stock allocation for a growth-oriented portfolio. The number inside each box represents the percentage of the stock type held in the portfolio. The left-hand column represents value stocks, and the right-hand column represents growth stocks. The style boxes show that the portfolio is leaning toward a growth strategy, as the heaviest weightings are on that side of the box.

While larger, more established companies may not grow as rapidly as some small or midsize companies, they also have less risk. Large, established companies have built such strong foundations in their business, they are less likely to go out of business or have their primary revenue sources lost to the competition. Smaller, growing companies rely on new product concepts, new technology, or new socioeconomic trends to gain market share for their company and increase sales and profits. Smaller companies need to take on a greater amount of debt to finance their growth. These high debt levels pose risks to investors. If the company can't grow sales and profits as expected, it may have difficulty paying down the debt. If the economy changes and interest rates start rising, the cost of debt will increase, which will cut into profits. On the flip side of the risk is the fact that companies like IBM and Apple were small cap stocks at one time. Due to their technological innovations, great vision into the future, and strong business strategies, they grew into giants, and investors who went along for the ride could have made millions.

While it's advisable to have small and mid cap stocks in a portfolio, *it's important to have the appropriate balance of stock types to manage risk.* Stock values can vary widely and may change based on many circumstances, including general economic trends, geopolitical changes, social trends, and company-specific trends such as earnings. Stock prices are highly unpredictable in most cases. It is for these reasons that diversification, and some degree of professional management, is necessary for you to be successful.

BONDS

Bond investments are referred to as "income securities." In layman's terms, bonds are a very formal version of an "I owe you." Essentially, they are debt instruments where investors can lend money to a corporation or government agency, receive the bond certificate (which spells out the terms of the loan) as a security, and then sell that bond on an open market for more or less than what the actual debt is. Of course, the bond holder can simply hold onto the bond, receive the promised interest payments over time, and then receive a payback of the loan amount from the company or government agency when the bond matures.

When you invest in a bond, you are promised a certain interest rate based on current yields at the time of the initial loan amount. This is called the *coupon rate*. The bond will have a stated term during which the debtor—the company or government agency that issued the bond—will pay the coupon rate and then return the original loan amount at maturity. Most corporate bonds have a fixed coupon rate. The bond provides the bondholder that interest rate every year in the form of a fixed dollar amount. If you have a $10,000 bond with a 5 percent coupon rate, that means you will receive $500 per year for ten years. That $500 amount remains fixed for the life of the bond. There are many variations of bonds. There are corporate bonds, government bonds, and municipal bonds. Although most bonds have a fixed coupon rate, there are some bonds that offer floating rates. There are different term bonds ranging from 1 or 2 years (short term), 5 to 10 years (intermediate term), and 20 to 30 years (long term).

Bonds are typically less volatile than stocks and thus may be more predictable in terms of returns. However, bond investments do have certain risks. It's important to identify what those risks are in order to understand how and when to invest in them. Bonds have two types of risk: *credit risk* and *interest rate risk*. Considering that you are lending money to a corporation, the first question you might ask before making this investment is, will they pay me back? This is referred to as credit risk, the risk of the corporation going out of business or filing chapter 11 bankruptcy and not paying back your loan. Government bonds are considered to be the safest from the possibility of credit risk. There has never been a bond issued by the US government that was not honored and paid at maturity. For corporate bonds, there are bond rating bureaus, such as Standard & Poor's, that help qualify which corporations are creditworthy and which have more credit risk. If you're investing in bond mutual funds in your 401(k), the fund fact sheet will indicate the quality of the bonds in the portfolio, AAA, AA, A, BBB, and so on. All bonds rated BBB and above are considered high-quality bonds. Some investors like investing in lower quality bonds because they pay higher interest rates in lieu of the credit risk you're taking to own them. These are called *high yield bonds* or *junk bonds*. From 2008 through 2011, there was a total of $7.4 trillion in corporate bonds outstanding in the United States. A total of 4.1 percent of those bonds were defaulted on (not paid or subject to reduced payment) as reported by Bloomberg and Bond Buyer effective 12/31/11. This includes both high quality and below grade, "junk" bonds.

The trick with bonds and bond mutual funds is to understand interest rate risk—the inverse relationship between bond values and interest rates. Because most bonds have a fixed rate (coupon rate), the yield on a bond could become more or less attractive if interest rates change. This could impact the value of your bond should you wish to sell it before it matures. To understand interest rate risk, let's assume you invest $10,000 in a new ten-year bond that has a 5 percent coupon rate and pays $500 per year. A year later, interest rates rise such that new bonds like yours are paying 7 percent. Your bond would not be an attractive investment to someone else. Should you wish to sell that bond, ultimately, you will need to lower the price so that the $500 payment would represent something closer to a 7 percent interest rate. Your bond value could drop below $9,000 in such a scenario. This discounted value is a result of interest rate risk. Because the bond will be worth the full $10,000 at maturity in 9 years, the amount of the discount is limited to reflect the appreciation in value the new bond investor will likely earn from the discount upon maturity. The combination of the coupon rate (interest) and the change in value of the bond from the purchase price to the face value at maturity is used to determine *yield to maturity*. If you are considering investing in an individual bond, the yield to maturity is the most important number relative to the true rate of return you can expect to receive. For bond mutual funds, you want to pay close attention to distribution rate, average credit quality, and the average maturity to gauge whether or not it's the right investment for you at that time.

Interest rate changes can also work in your favor if you're a bond investor. Consider the opposite scenario.

You've been fortunate to put a sizable portion of your investments into a money market while interest rates have been rising. You can see that interest rates are at 8 percent or higher. You decide it's a good time to own bonds, and you invest in a long-term bond fund. As interest rates drop back to historical averages, your bond values may go up considerably. While you wait, your investment is yielding high returns relative to current interest rates. Obviously, the best time to invest in bonds is when interest rates are high or going down. The riskiest time to invest in bonds is when interest rates are low and rising. When interest rates are low, focus your fixed income investments in bonds with short-term maturities. When interest rates are high, enjoy the benefit of longer-term bonds, and lock in higher coupon rates.

MONEY MARKETS, CDS, AND CASH EQUIVALENTS

Investing in cash equivalents is usually reserved for the portion of your portfolio that you want anchored in safety without as much concern for earnings. This would also be a place for funds that you wish to remain liquid for near term use or reinvestment once the opportunity arises. In times when the economy is struggling or the markets are experiencing volatility, you may simply want a safe haven to hold your money in until the storm clears.

A money market is a mutual fund made up of very short-term bonds or notes. These notes are an essential component of our economy, as they facilitate the flow of capital through the economy. Companies can routinely borrow money from large financial institutions for 7 days, 15 days, or a month, and because these notes are for such short terms, your investment in the fund is liquid. Interest rates on these ultra short-term notes will be based mostly on the Federal Reserve's established short-term rates that in 2014 are near zero.

For this reason, there are alternative investments for safe money, such as stable value funds, that are usually liquid like a money market but offer more attractive returns because they incorporate guaranteed interest contracts (GICs) into their portfolio. A bank CD is a type of guaranteed interest contract. The bank offers you a promised interest rate so long as you promise to place your money with them for a stated period. GICs are used by large financial institutions like banks and insurance companies as a type of interest bearing note to offer to large-scale investors in return for the use of their money, the same way a bank does business with you when you put money in a CD. The bank then uses your money to lend out to borrowers at higher interest rates.

Money markets and GICs are types of cash equivalents—investments that are very low risk, liquid, and offering to return current short-term interest rates. When rates are low, seek stable value funds (GICs). When interest rates are rising, seek money markets.

COMMODITIES

Investors should not be afraid of commodities. In fact, commodities are easy to understand compared to most other investments. *Commodities are the things that we use in our everyday life such as food, energy, timber, industrial-use metal, and gold.* Consider commodities to be hard assets with a constant value while the value of cash can fluctuate under various economic circumstances such as inflation. Essentially, if it now costs you $200 to buy the same materials or energy products that cost only $150 last year, the value of your dollar has gone down by some 25 percent. Conversely, if you invested that $150 last year in these products, they would have increased in value by 33 percent. This is based on the fact that $150 worth of these products one year ago is now worth $200. Therefore, the value of your investment has increased by $50. The products themselves are the same, and they serve the same purpose. So the buying power of your dollar has decreased, but because you invested in these products, you have hedged your dollars against the adverse effects of inflation. If put another way, the value of materials or food commodities in terms of dollars has gone up. If the cost of wood is rising, then the investor owning timber is seeing an appreciation for the value of his investment. If oil prices increase by 10 percent, the owner of a barrel of oil has seen his or her asset go up in value by 10 percent. Investing in commodities can be a great hedge against inflation, because as prices of goods rise, so will the value of most commodities and thus, the value of your investment.

There are other factors affecting commodity prices, such as increases or decreases in demand for certain products, the scarcity of natural resources, or variations in currency values. Like stock investments, there are many elements of commodity investing that are unpredictable, such as global economic changes. This is why investors would be wise to invest in a commodity index fund that offers a broad approach to the commodity markets. Your 401(k) may offer ETFs that focus on energy, natural resources, or precious metals, and each of these investment styles has its own set of risk and reward considerations. If you're not an astute commodity investor, the easiest choice would be a broad-based commodity index fund. *Simply put, commodities are a very good way to hedge a portfolio from the adverse effects of inflation.*

ACTION ITEMS

Review your current investments and make an effort to identify the types of stocks (value, growth, small cap, large cap, and so on) you hold. Identify your bonds based on length of time to maturity and credit quality. Check whether your portfolio is truly balanced and if it is in fact diversified. Do you own hard assets such as real estate or commodities?

If you're not comfortable reallocating your portfolio to be diversified, seek the assistance of a financial advisor.

TACTICAL ASSET ALLOCATION

It is unusual for retirement plans to offer tactical asset allocation services. However, making modest adjustments to your portfolio when economic conditions change can help you buffer your assets from the effects of negative market trends. The difference between market timing and tactical asset allocation is that with tactical asset allocation, you only move small segments of your portfolio at any given time. For example, let's assume that you determine the stock market is at an all-time high. There's been a bull market ongoing for five years, and you believe the market may be nearing its peak. You'd like to protect your profits before the next bear market. A tactical move would be to reduce your equity position by ten percentage points. So, an aggressive investor would reduce stocks from 90 percent to 80 percent or possibly adjust their portfolio risk down one level to the moderate growth level of 75 percent stock. This is a tactical adjustment. Another type of tactical change would be relative to economic conditions such as inflation or rising interest rates. In these cases, you may determine that the economy may see rising inflation, which is generally not good for stocks, as higher prices may force consumers to buy fewer goods. You now know that commodities tend to perform well in inflationary economies, as they often increase in value as the prices for those goods increase. A tactical adjustment might be to reduce your stock holdings and reallocate those funds into a commodity index fund. If you're an aggressive investor, you may even choose precious metals as your commodity.

Tactical Asset Allocation is a strategy whereby you make only modest adjustments to a portfolio based on the current circumstances. If it turns out that your tactical adjustment didn't work, it will not have a devastating effect, because it only impacts a relatively small percentage of your portfolio. If the tactical adjustment is timely and correct, it may result in increased returns. In fact, tactical asset allocation may enable you to enhance returns over time by reducing the negative impact of bearish market trends on your portfolio. If you have the time and the right advice to stay on top of the economic trends, tactical portfolio adjustments should be made in incremental steps. I suggest that in order to limit the adverse effects of market timing, you limit portfolio adjustments to shifts of no more than 10 percent of your portfolio at any one time and no more than 20 to 25 percent in total variance from your original asset allocation.

For example, let's say you're 40 years old, and you are seeking long-term growth as your investment objective. You are not opposed to investment risk, but you desire to have some balance in the portfolio to moderate volatility and at the same time have an age-appropriate investment strategy. You've determined that your ideal portfolio style would be a moderate growth model. An example of a moderate growth portfolio is as follows:

Large cap stock	33 percent
Mid cap stock	14 percent
Small cap stock	10 percent
Foreign stock	18 percent
Multi-sector bonds	10 percent
Intermediate bonds	10 percent
Money market	5 percent

This basic portfolio design consists of 75 percent stock, 20 percent bonds, and 5 percent money market (cash equivalent). The range of change to your asset allocation strategy in a tactical adjustment would be to (gradually) reduce your stock positions from 75 percent to a low of 50 percent during times of poor stock market performance or your perception thereof. Should you make such a shift, you could reallocate those dollars to bonds, cash, or commodities. For example, you see that interest rates are on the rise, and you are concerned that the economy is going to suffer. As a result, the stock market may perform negatively, and bond values may be subject to interest rate risk. The first change you can make is to move your long- and intermediate-term bonds to short-term bonds, floating rate bonds, and/or money market. This will reduce your interest rate risk without changing the percentage allocation to bonds and cash from the current 25 percent level. Next, you might shift 10 percent out of your stock positions and reallocate the money to commodities. In this example, you've made two tactical changes with only a 10 percent shift in equity exposure.

Now let's assume that your projections were correct—six months later interest rates are rising more dramatically, and stocks have been more volatile. You've been advised that small cap and mid cap stocks rely heavily on debt to finance operations, and with higher interest rates their costs would be higher. This will squeeze profits. You're concerned about inflation and the overall condition of the economy. As a result, you decide to make a second shift and sell off ten percent of your small cap and mid cap stocks. This time you simply put the proceeds in the money market to earn short-term yields and wait for an opportunity to reinvest in bonds at higher interest rates or back into stocks at a later date. These would be examples of tactical adjustments to your portfolio that are designed to buffer the effects of adverse economic conditions while avoiding the risk of outright market timing.

It's easy to argue that if you have the data to suggest that reallocating your portfolio is advisable, then you should simply go ahead and shift everything accordingly. The problem comes in where reality meets theory. Reality *always* wins. The reality is that no one knows for sure how far economic trends will go and/or when they will turn around. So even if you're spot on with the idea of reducing stock in favor of bonds or cash, when will you reallocate those assets back to the original allocation to take advantage of the market rebound? Most investors are unsure, and as a result, they tend to allow emotion to cloud their judgment, which often results in sitting on the sidelines too long while the market rebounds. For this reason, it is very dangerous to make wholesale changes to your asset allocation, as this could preclude you from participating in some of the best stock market performances over time. The idea is to make adjustments when markets are less favorable to avoid substantial declines but limit those adjustments so you can retain positions in the markets to participate in the upside. When the investment markets begin to rise again, it will be relatively easy to reinvest in your original asset allocation strategy.

RULES OF THUMB

Here are some basic rules of thumb for portfolio management.

- Rising interest rates are detrimental to bonds in general.
- The later the maturity date of the bonds you hold, the more interest rate risk you have as interest rates rise.
- When rates are very low, shorter-term bonds and floating rate bonds are more attractive.

- Inflation is also bad for bonds, as that usually results in higher interest rates.

- In periods of rising interest rates, it is wise to reduce bond holdings and shift those funds to money market or fixed-rate accounts.

- Money markets offer safety and increasing rates, whereas bonds may lose value.

When interest rates are high, you should invest in long-term bonds. They will offer attractive returns as long as rates are high and likely appreciate in value should interest rates go down.

Rising interest rates may also adversely affect stocks, although this scenario is not as simple. The stock market does not like high interest rates or inflation rates that are higher than the average 3-4 percent per year. High interest rates cut into corporate profits, particularly those of smaller, growing companies that use greater amounts of debt to finance their operations. High inflation indicates economic problems such as a recession.

During inflationary periods, the cost of goods rises faster than the income level of the average consumer. This differential makes it harder for people to afford purchasing the same goods and services. As prices rise, consumer demand tends to go down. As fewer goods and services are purchased, corporate profits are squeezed. Corporations then raise prices to maintain profitability while cutting production and jobs. It's a vicious cycle, which is why it can take years to unravel. During economic periods such as this, it may be prudent to increase the percentage of your portfolio held in commodities and money markets and reduce the percentage held in small cap and mid cap stocks.

There's an old saying: "When rates are high, stocks will die. When rates are low, stocks will grow."

Below is a table of historic inflation rates as reported by Inflation-Data.com. As you can see, the last decade has had an average annual inflation rate of only 2.43 percent. This represents the lowest decade average in 30 years and is well below the historic average inflation rate of 3.1 percent in the United States. I believe we could see a return to normal, if not higher-than-average inflation rates in the next decade. This may cause investors to look closely at their portfolio strategy.

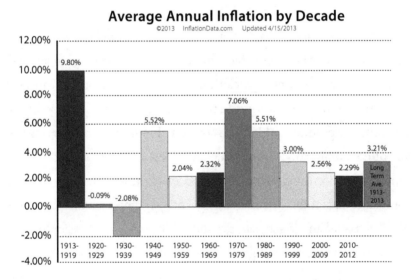

The effects of above average inflation on stocks are typically quite negative. In the short term, however, inflation can have a positive effect on certain stocks, such as those of companies who own or control commodities and natural resources. *Hard assets* are things like timberland, real estate, and precious metals. *Natural resources* would include oil and natural gas, minerals, and naturally occurring food products. *Commodities* and commodity-based businesses are attractive areas to invest in place of traditional stock funds during periods of inflation.

Knowing which of the aforementioned investments to minimize or allocate more money to in various economic circumstances can make a definitive difference in your results and keep you positioned for positive returns. Making minor adjustments to the mix of stocks, bonds, cash, and commodities in your portfolio can help you reduce losses without taking you out of the game when the markets reverse direction. For those investors who are not confident in the knowledge of what portfolio strategies to employ during changing economic conditions, I recommend that you seek the advice of a *registered investment advisor* (RIA) to monitor your investments and advise you on your investment allocation strategy.

It may be valuable to understand the meaning of defensive investing. Investing in stocks of companies that produce necessities such as food, health care products, energy, clothing, and natural resources can be a good way to minimize downside risk. These are stocks of corporations that produce products that will be consumed in similar amounts regardless of economic conditions. They are called *consumer defensive stocks*. One of the nice things about this kind of stock is that many of these companies are quite well established and pay good dividends. Those dividends offer an attractive buffer should the stock market go down or simply tread water and not go up during economic struggles.

Some 401(k) plans will allow participants to open an outside brokerage account as part of their investment portfolio. If you consider investing in individual stocks, I submit that a portfolio of dividend paying stocks from consumer defensive industries offers an attractive strategy. They can offer a degree of stability that most other stocks do not. This degree of safety comes from the nature of their business. Large, well-established companies in the food, health care, energy, and utility industries will continue to be able to sell their products in increasing amounts, as these items are essential for survival. As the population grows, so does their market, regardless of the economy.

Often stocks of the largest blue chip companies pay dividends. Dividends are a share of company profits that investors can participate in. This is in addition to the opportunity for capital appreciation in the stock. Dividends also serve a defensive role. They provide you with income to offset some of the negative effects of market downturns. Often the opportunity to receive those stated dividend yields could help support the stock price and reduce volatility in downward markets. They can also provide you with a way to buy low if dividends are reinvested during market declines. Considering the added risk of investing in individual stocks, it may be best to look for a good dividend income fund to have in your portfolio. You can choose a managed fund such as a mutual fund or an index of dividend stocks through an ETF.

Another example of defensive investing that has been followed for many years is called the "Dogs of the Dow." This strategy calls for investing in the ten highest dividend-yielding stocks among the 30 Dow Jones Industrial Average stocks. The theory is based, in part, on the idea that above average dividend yields from some of the largest and most established corporations in the United States would reduce volatility. The theory also assumes that these ten stocks may have performed the worst among the group of Dow stocks (which is in part the reason for their above average dividend yield), and these companies may present the opportunity to rebound. Investors in the Dogs of the Dow can enjoy above average dividend yields while they wait for their stocks to appreciate.

The table below illustrates the Dogs of the Dow for 2014. The term "Small Dog" indicates the five lowest priced stocks among the group.

DOGS OF DOW TABLE

NYSE / NASDAQ	Company the Dow stocks ranked by yield on 12/31/14	Price on 12/31/14	Yield on 12/31/14	Small Dog on 12/31/14
T	AT&T	33.59	5.48%	Yes
VZ	Verizon	46.78	4.70%	Yes
CVX	Chevron	112.18	3.82%	No
MCD	McDonlad's	93.70	3.63%	No
PFE	Pfizer	31.15	3.60%	Yes
GE	General Electric	25.27	3.48%	Yes
MRK	Merck	56.79	3.17%	No
CAT	Caterpillar	91.53	3.06%	No
XOM	ExxonMobil	92.45	2.99%	No
KO	Coca-Cola	42.22	2.89%	Yes

Source: www.dogsofthedow.com

The average dividend yield for this group is 3.88 percent, which compared to current interest rates would represent a very attractive yield in 2015. The next table illustrates the complete list of the stocks making up the Dow Jones Industrial Average.

Symbol NYSE / NASDAQ	Company the 2015 Dogs of the Dow are listed in gray	Price on 12/31/14	Yield on 12/31/14
T	AT&T	33.59	5.48%
VZ	Verizon	46.78	4.7%

CVX	Chevron	112.18	3.82%
MCD	McDonald's	93.70	3.63%
PFE	Pfizer	31.15	3.60%
GE	General Electric	25.27	3.48%
MRK	Merck	56.79	3.17%
CAT	Caterpillar	91.53	3.06%
XOM	ExxonMobil	92.45	2.99%
KO	Coca-Cola	42.22	2.89%
PG	Procter & Gamble	91.09	2.82%
IBM	International Business Machines	160.44	2.74%
CSCO	Cisco Systems	27.82	2.73%
JNJ	Johnson & Johnson	104.57	2.68%
MSFT	Microsoft	46.45	2.67%
JPM	JP Morgan Chase	62.58	2.56%
DD	DuPont	73.94	2.54%
INTC	Intel	36.29	2.48%
BA	Boeing	129.98	2.25%
WMT	Wal-Mart	85.88	2.24%
MMM	3M	164.32	2.08%
TRV	The Travelers Companies	105.85	2.08%
UTX	United Technologies	115.00	2.05%
HD	Home Depot	104.97	1.79%
UNH	UnitedHealth Group	101.09	1.48%
DIS	Disney	94.19	1.22%
NKE	Nike	96.15	1.16%
GS	Goldman Sachs	193.83	1.14%
AXP	American Express	93.04	1.12%
V	Visa	65.55	0.73%

Source: www.dogsofthedow.com

Investing in individual stocks involves above average risk and may not be advisable for every 401(k) plan investor. Please consult a financial advisor, and consider the value of extensive research before investing. If you are to consider investing a portion of your retirement fund in an outside brokerage account, start with a relatively small percentage of your total assets. Compare the results of your outside brokerage account with your mutual funds and ETFs over time to determine which investment strategy is working best for you.

ACTION ITEMS

Consider the definition of tactical asset allocation and what it takes for this to be a successful strategy. If you determine if this is a course you wish to follow, consider the need for professional guidance and interview investment advisors to find the person with whom you are most comfortable.

With these concepts in mind and with the understanding and acceptance that market timing can be dangerous, proceed with caution! Seek the assistance of a financial advisor before reallocating. Always remember that one option you have is to do nothing and keep your portfolio intact.

Sometimes it is as valuable to know when change is warranted as it is to know what change to make. Let a professional guide you. It's usually worth the fee you pay if the advisor is well qualified.

CHAPTER 8

FIDUCIARY OBLIGATIONS AND BEST PRACTICES FOR PLAN SPONSORS

FIDUCIARY OBLIGATIONS

There is a great misconception among small businesses of what fiduciary responsibility actually means relative to 401(k) plan sponsorship. Most businesspeople assume that their vendor is responsible for compliance with ERISA and the fulfillment of the fiduciary role. It is most often quite the contrary.

The US legislature is determined to further define the role of the ERISA fiduciary and who will be held to that standard. It has been said that an ERISA fiduciary has the highest standard of responsibility under the law. Whereas the definition of general fiduciary care is based on the prudent man rule, the definition of an ERISA fiduciary is based on the prudent expert rule. In short, an ERISA fiduciary has a responsibility to be sufficiently astute in his or her knowledge of the ERISA regulations to carry them out with particular care and efficiency. The absence of that ability does not absolve a plan sponsor from the resulting liability.

The fundamental truth in 401(k) plan management is that the plan sponsor bears the primary, if not the entire responsibility for ERISA compliance, IRS compliance, and any matter of human resources law relative to employee benefit plan offerings. ERISA regulations state that hiring a third party to conduct plan administration or provide investment advice or fiduciary services is prohibited—that is, unless the services in question are deemed "necessary" for proper management of the plan and the fees charged for such services are "reasonable." Clearly a plan sponsor can establish that engaging a third party is necessary to assure that their plan is administered properly given the complexity of the rules governing 401(k) plans as well as the various communications, document restatements, calculations, and testing requirements to remain compliant. Similarly, given that most business owners and their employees are not investment professionals, it stands to reason that hiring an outside fiduciary to manage the plan investments as well as overall compliance oversight would be deemed necessary. The larger and more difficult question is whether or not the fees charged for these services are reasonable as defined by ERISA.

Although fiduciary responsibility for 401(k) and other qualified retirement plans initially rests with the plan sponsor (the employer), there are registered investment advisors and ERISA attorneys who may be hired as a "named fiduciary" for your plan. However, the plan sponsor is never completely absolved of responsibility for compliance with the rules affecting qualified retirement plans or the potential liability arising from fiduciary shortcomings. Having a qualified named fiduciary for your retirement plan provides you with a protective blanket against the storm of IRS and Department of Labor auditors out there every day looking at plans like yours under a microscope. The essence of a named fiduciary is that they are literally part of your team and sit on the same side of the table as you do when it comes to being responsible for proper plan management. Because of this relationship, they have a vested interest in your success. Their first objective will be to design and deliver the highest quality retirement plan to your participants. *This is the first step in insulating yourself from liability.*

The plan sponsor must exercise due diligence in selecting a named fiduciary and any other vendor that provides services to the plan. That due diligence would include

- Verifying the credentials of the proposed providers;

- Reviewing their services and their success in delivering those services timely; and

- Researching whether the providers have had notable violations or sanctions from governing bodies such as the Securities & Exchange Commission (SEC).

In selecting service providers to act as a fiduciary for your plan, you should look for the following credentials:

REGISTERED INVESTMENT ADVISOR

A registered investment advisor (RIA) is typically an independent advisor governed under the auspices of the SEC. These advisors generally charge fees to provide unbiased, research-based investment advice, as opposed to being paid a commission to sell an investment product. While this sounds like a simple distinction, there are several very important concerns with commission-based investments in 401(k) plans. First, it is recognized by ERISA that commission-based programs may create a conflict of interest for a broker providing advice to the plan sponsor where certain investments provide more or less compensation than others. Second, commission-based investment models and prepackaged investment products tend to preclude access to many of the lowest cost investments, such as ETFs, and generally limit the plan manager's investment alternatives to a small segment of the universe of choices. This limitation itself presents a conflict of interest to a commission-based broker and may prevent the plan sponsor from meeting the necessary fiduciary standards in managing their retirement plan (see Tibble vs. Edison). Typically, commission-based arrangements preclude the broker from being a named fiduciary for an ERISA retirement plan such as a 401(k) plan under current law.

There can be numerous advantages to having a fee-based advisor assisting a plan sponsor with the investment selection and monitoring process. The standards by which an RIA is governed indicate that he or she must exercise due diligence in selecting investments to recommend for his or her clients, and the selection process must be conducted in a fiduciary capacity. In other words, by the very nature of their credential, they are a fiduciary in the management of their clients' investments. This same edict of high fiduciary standards, which is inherently required in the management of your 401(k) plan, gives rise to the RIA being well qualified to act as a named fiduciary for your plan.

ACCREDITED INVESTMENT FIDUCIARY

An accredited investment fiduciary has completed extensive training in fiduciary standards established for providing investment advice to 401(k) plans and other qualified retirement plans. This accreditation allows the plan sponsor to engage a professional with a documented background which provides the standard of education and training that can be expected from the service provider. Thus, an element of due diligence has been established to protect the plan sponsor.

CERTIFIED FINANCIAL ANALYST

A certified financial analyst (CFA) possesses the technical skills to evaluate investment alternatives in a scientific way, typically incorporating economic data with data from complex analytic systems to form judgments about which investments will fare best under the current circumstances. CFAs will also use this data to make recommendations for investment fund choices in your plan. They also extend a great degree of effort in analyzing and monitoring your investment choices, asset allocation models, and market trends on an ongoing basis. The value of a CFA to your 401(k) plan is that they will provide logical and scientific support for investment decisions made on behalf of the plan, thus establishing and maintaining high standards of fiduciary care in the investment selection process for your retirement plan.

ERISA ATTORNEY

An employer may retain the services of an ERISA attorney to oversee the management of the plan. Certain attorneys will offer named fiduciary services to plan sponsors for a fee. The strength of the ERISA attorney relationship is that they can provide legal advice, draft custom plan documents, and research legal remedies to problems that may arise with your plan. However, given the cost of hiring an attorney and the fact that they generally do not provide investment advice, most plan sponsors choose to seek fiduciary assistance through their investment advisor and hire an attorney only when needed.

Your proposed third party fiduciary should offer a written scope of services detailing their obligations to the plan in the form of a service agreement so that you know what you can expect for the fees being charged. This would become a valuable tool for recourse against the named fiduciary should there be a liability arising out of a breach of fiduciary duties. Having the full scope of services documented also serves to satisfy your obligation under ERISA Sect. 408(b)(2) to have full knowledge of services being rendered for any fees being charged to the plan.

Each provider should substantiate their credentials to act in the stated capacity for the plan. For example, ERISA specifies the role and responsibilities of a named fiduciary in sections 3(21)(a)(ii) and 3(38) as well as indicating guidelines for compensation of such fiduciaries in section 408(b)(2). Finally, you should verify that your third party fiduciary maintains an ERISA bond as well as adequate insurance for errors and omissions.

With all this detail to consider in selecting a third party fiduciary for your 401(k) plan, one might ask if it would be simpler to buy a guidebook and simply follow the directions. Unfortunately, that would just make things difficult! *The bottom line in hiring the right professional(s) to act as a fiduciary on behalf of your plan is that they will bear the lion's share of responsibility for keeping your plan in compliance with all IRS and ERISA regulations.* In most cases, the net impact on plan costs is negligible, if it increases costs at all. The basis on which you may expect to retain these unbiased services at no incremental increase in cost is that a registered investment advisor will look to incorporate ETFs and low cost index-based mutual funds into your 401(k) plan. This type of investment fund offers the investor the option to invest in a market index at nearly one-quarter the cost (on average) of a traditional managed mutual fund. This integration of low-cost investments will bring your plan's weighted average investment expense down considerably.

The typical business owner and/or HR professional may have trouble fully understanding the complex nature of the IRS and ERISA provisions particularly, as well as following the frequent rule changes. Further, a properly credentialed fiduciary will proactively advise you of legislative changes that may affect your plan or require you to take action to maintain compliance.

Consider that the Department of Labor has ten regional offices in the United States and the primary purpose of each office is to audit ERISA-qualified retirement plans. These ten offices collectively attempt to audit some 5,000 plans per year. The sole objective of these offices is to raise revenue through sanctions against employers for retirement plan compliance failures. The IRS also audits retirement plans from a tax law perspective and does so with the same goal of generating revenue for our heavy-spending government. If your plan becomes subject to sanctions or a lawsuit arising out of a fiduciary failure, your named fiduciary will be on the hook along with you. Chances are they will have taken steps to preclude such a liability from occurring.

ACTION ITEMS

Conduct periodic due diligence in the form of fee bench-marking for all expenses charged to the plan, including investment expenses and management fees. Obtain an independent analysis of your plan costs that will compare them to a benchmark average and to competitive alternatives to determine if your plan fees are reasonable by ERISA standards. Assess the services being rendered for those fees, and assure that they are necessary. Do this by verifying that each party receiving compensation is providing a valuable service to the plan and/or the plan participants. Evaluate their respective services for timeliness, accuracy, and completeness, and document your reviews so that they may be presented to the Department of Labor or the IRS should your plan be audited.

BIG BROTHER

From 2001 to 2012 the IRS and the Department of Labor have made eight significant legislative changes to qualified retirement plan (QRP) rules and regulations: an average of one new law every 1.37 years!

What many employers find most challenging is keeping track of all of the documentation required by these legislative changes. It is common when new legislation is put into law that a time frame for compliance with the new regulation is established. Ironically, it's not uncommon for the law itself to be incomplete and/or subject to final interpretation at the time when the initial notice and timeline are established. This usually results in the timeline being pushed back once, twice, or even three times. At some point down the road, the final regulations are determined, and the drop-dead date for compliance is established. For example, the Pension Protection Act of 2006 was not completed until 2007!

The recent ERISA Sect. 408(b)(2) legislation requiring fee disclosure was originally slated to take effect in 2011 in two phases. The first phase was vendor disclosures to employers. The second phase was the employer disclosure to participants. With all the back and forth among lawyers trying to nail down the meaning of the law, the Department of Labor realized that it was a virtual impossibility for vendors to comply in time. So the deadline was changed.

RECENT 401K LEGISLATION

- EGTRRA - Economic Growth and Tax Relief Reconciliation Act (2001)
- Sarbanese-Oxley (2002)
- Savers Tax Credit (2002)
- G.U.S.T. (2003)
- Pension Protection Act (2006-07)
- WRERA (2010)
- HEART Amendment (2010)
- ERISA 408(b)(2) (2011-12)

In spite of all of these changes, there is yet a new frontier of legislative efforts coming in 2015 and beyond. This new round of regulatory changes will focus on the retirement readiness of the participants and what plan sponsors and record keepers should be responsible to do to improve the rate of success among their plan participants. In 2012, Senator Thomas Harkin of Iowa stated that the current shortfall among workers in the United States for their collective retirement income needs is $6.7 trillion! The fed knows there is a retirement crisis in this country and that Social Security can't solve it.

The most recent piece of legislation affecting retirement plans was ERISA 408(b)(2), which took effect in 2012. This is one of the most significant legislative changes in the past decade, as it augments many of the most fundamental ERISA standards into a complex and cumbersome fee-disclosure requirement for plan sponsors. Once again, this law was initially passed in late 2010 with the originally intended effective date being June 30, 2011. Given the magnitude of the new responsibilities placed on plan sponsors, record keepers, and investment companies, and a lack of clarity of exactly what documentation constituted compliance with the law, the Department of Labor extended the effective date to January 1, 2012, then extended the date for full compliance to August 30, 2012.

This single piece of legislation has permanently changed the landscape of 401(k) plans for the better, although it is a difficult challenge for plan sponsors to maintain the fiduciary standards it imposes. Why do I say for the better? The requirement for fee disclosure on the part of investment companies or insurance companies selling packaged products brings out into the open what have long been hidden expenses that plan participants had no way of understanding. Moreover, plan sponsors themselves were often in the dark as to what the true costs of their plan have been and thus could not take effective action to manage those costs. One might imagine the abuses that may have taken place by certain vendors. Clearly, the new fee transparency rules will force vendors to sharpen their pencils and cut out excess fees or be exposed as not being worthy to provide 401(k) products competitively.

Consider the essence of the law as it relates to the obligations of the plan sponsor. Initially, it may sound relatively simple. However, there are far-reaching implications of strict fiduciary standards that may leave any plan sponsor exposed to sanctions resulting from a plan audit or legal obligations resulting from a lawsuit. The three fundamental requirements for a plan sponsor are:

- Identify all plan expenses and the specific services being rendered/received for those costs. Assure that those services are necessary for the proper operation of the plan.

- Assess the level of costs to determine if they are reasonable and competitive in the marketplace.

- Disclose these fees in writing to all plan participants in the form of an annual disclosure schedule and the actual expenditures (in dollars) for each plan participant periodically.

In light of this regulatory environment, it's quite clear that there is a necessity for outside vendors to provide assistance in managing your plan. The challenge comes in determining whether or not your plan expenses are "reasonable." The absence of that determination is where the fiduciary liability may exist. Plan sponsors have an obligation not only to hire vendors to provide services but to assure that those services are delivered timely, completely, and at a cost that is competitive relative to other plans of similar size and scope. Essentially, a periodic benchmarking of your service providers' fees and services is necessary. Therefore, an independent service provider who can deliver this reporting is another essential service for the proper operation of the plan and to preclude fiduciary failure on the part of the plan sponsor.

In 2010, the Department of Labor (DOL) doubled its auditing force nationwide with the sole intent of deriving increased revenue in the form of sanctions on plan sponsors who may have various fiduciary shortfalls in meeting ERISA guidelines. With the DOL and the IRS aggressively auditing thousands of employer plans every year, employers should be aware that DOL and IRS audits can require an employer to produce any and all documentation, legislative amendments, and financial information for their plan from the initial effective date of their 401(k) plan. Unlike personal audits, which can only incorporate the last years, there is no statute of limitation! Failure to produce all requested documentation may result in the disqualification of your plan. Any failure to have properly executed the adoption of all required legislative changes or to maintain the required documentation will result in the potential disqualification of your plan or hefty fines.

When a plan is disqualified for a failure to be compliant or a failure to have remained (continuously) compliant, the results could be quite disruptive and damaging. In the case of a plan that is ultimately disqualified without resolution, the total contributions made to the plan for the prior two to three years (possibly as far back in time as the violation occurred for more egregious acts) can be nullified and refunded to participants and employers. This would also include a reversal of all tax benefits associated with those contributions! Recognizing that this action would not be in the best interest of the plan participants, the IRS or Department of Labor tends to offer a "voluntary compliance resolution" (VCR) program as a corrective process for deficient plans and noncompliant plan sponsors. This process, of course, is coupled with fines and sanctions against the employer as a slap on the hand for their supposed failures. In 2013, the Department of Labor collected fines of over $1.6 billion. This represents a 33 percent increase from the $1.2 billion tallied in 2012.

THE LAW AND RETIREMENT PLANS

CASE STUDY

A prominent company in the Boston area that maintains a 401(k) plan (we'll call them "Mr. Flowers Co.") recently received a notice from the IRS that their 401(k) plan would be audited. The notice stated that the audit request was based on random selection and gave an extensive list of documentation that the IRS intended to review as part of their process. As a named fiduciary for the plan, I was very much involved in the data and document compilation required, as well as being present in all meetings with the IRS agent at the plan sponsor's executive offices. In the IRS notice to the plan sponsor, they requested every plan document and plan amendment for the prior ten years. Interestingly, unlike personal income tax audits, where the IRS can only review the last 7 years, a 401(k) audit has no statute of limitations, and the IRS can request plan documentation dating as far back as the origination of the plan.

One of the difficulties that this request presented by seeking documentation that was up to ten years old is that we were required to seek information from vendors and plan administrators who had long since been replaced. The 401(k) plan was set up through a mutual fund company in 1997. We'll call it the XYZ Fund Company. I was hired by the firm to represent their interests in 2003. Due to their dissatisfaction with the current 401(k) vendor, we moved the investments and plan administration away from XYZ Fund Company to the ABC Mutual Fund Company. The reasons for the change included lower fees, more flexibility, and a wider selection of investment choices. Given the sheer volume of documentation required and given that the 2001–2003 period was wrought with major legislative changes and document amendments, it was very difficult for us to comply with the IRS audit requests based on the information the employer had on file.

Fortunately, the IRS gave us a reasonable amount of time to gather all of the required documentation. Also fortunate was that Mr. Flowers kept very good records and had most of the documents saved electronically on their server. However, given the volume of data requested and the age of much of the documentation, there were pieces that my client didn't have, and while my office provided the missing pieces from 2003 on (the period from which we began management), there were still some things from 2001–2003 we could not locate. At that point, we submitted everything we had to the IRS and noted we were still compiling some of the documentation through our 401(k) plan administrator. We were then forced to rely on information requested from the XYZ Fund Company, the former vendor, in order to complete the documentation required by the IRS.

One of the initial problems the IRS had with the plan documents we submitted was that many of them were not signed. *All plan documents must be signed, or they are considered invalid.* Unfortunately, most of the electronically saved documents were not signed copies. The electronic versions were simply the original documents that had likely been provided via email. Copies of the signed documents still needed to be located. So the staff at Mr. Flowers painstakingly dug through archived files to locate the signed documents. My office proceeded to work with the former plan administrator at XYZ Fund Company to gather the many missing documents from the early 2000s. Once we had all this compiled, we made a final submission to the IRS for them to prepare for their audit.

Needless to say, trying to get a former vendor to provide assistance of this type after nearly ten years had passed since we fired them was not easy. What was even more difficult was to get that vendor to explain many of their actions for plan amendments and restatements that were required actions at that point in time. This is where the IRS tried to hang us!

The scheduled IRS visit was known for some time as we desperately searched for every last item on their list. Prior to the meeting, I had several extensive conversations with the leaders and staff at Mr. Flowers Co., explaining what they should expect from the visit, where the IRS may try to find fault, and how we should conduct ourselves as a group in responding to the IRS agent's inquiries. When the day came, I was present in the meeting with the IRS agent and two HR staff people from Mr. Flowers Co., Jane and Kathy. The IRS agent began by reading through the plan adoption agreement and basic plan document. He went through each section in the adoption agreement and questioned certain provisions to ascertain if there were any violations in plan design. Immediately he referred to the eligibility section, where he stated that the plan's eligibility as written was not allowed. Therefore, the plan was disqualified.

Jane, the HR person to my left, turned white as a ghost and began leaning to one side as if she was falling off her chair. She stuttered as she was falling, and I quickly grabbed her arm and interjected, "Let me review the provision, and I might be able to explain." Once Jane was upright in her chair, I offered her some coffee and proceeded to read the eligibility guidelines in the adoption agreement.

On the surface, the eligibility provision appeared to say that a new employee was eligible after six months of employment and the completion of 1,000 hours of service within that period. The IRS agent claimed that this was invalid, because the rule states that in order to have a "minimum hours worked requirement," the eligibility period must be one year. For eligibility periods of less than one year, there can be no hours worked required to satisfy eligibility. This fundamental rule is, of course, true. However, in spite of the fact that I knew this and the IRS agent was giving me a headache, I calmly read through the provision, knowing that there was more to it than that.

I pointed out to the IRS agent that the provision actually was based on a full one year of service requirement with a minimum of 1,000 hours worked, but the plan allowed employees to enter in as few as six months once they've completed that 1,000-hour requirement. The IRS agent paused for a moment and then dropped his head as if he was just handed the losing decision in a boxing match. Slowly, he agreed that the provision as stated was permissible.

This type of exchange recurred as the agent went through the provisions of the plan. The meeting ended with him stating that he was going back to his office to review all of the documentation further and get back to us with his findings.

Approximately one month later, Mr. Flowers Co. received a letter from the IRS declaring that their plan was disqualified. The disqualification was based on their supposed failure to file an amendment, due in 2001, in a timely manner. In other words, the proper amendment had been filed, but in the IRS's opinion it was filed late, and as a result the plan was disqualified! So after ten years of spotless and accurate plan management and in spite of every element of their plan being perfectly documented and processed, the plan was to be disqualified because an extension form was filed late. For the record, if a 401(k) plan is disqualified, the repercussions are quite significant. The last two to three years of employee and corporate contributions must be reversed and all tax benefits lost. This is on top of the fact that the plan would be closed, and the IRS may not allow the employer to reopen a plan.

What makes this more convoluted is the nature of the documentation required back in 2001. The fact is that with the passage of the Economic Growth & Tax Relief Reconciliation Act in 2001 came significant changes to retirement plans, including a schedule for increased contribution limits over time. With two additional legislative changes to the 401(k) regulations in 2002 ("Sarbanes-Oxley" and "Savers Tax Credit"), the IRS created the GUST amendment, which required all employers to restate their entire plan document to incorporate all of the recent legislative amendments. Given that the IRS established an aggressive time line for compliance while the requirements of the law were still being interpreted, they decided to extend the deadline for compliance to allow businesses to extend the period for filing the amended plan document. This extension (called the GUST remedial amendment period) required employers to file an extension form to elect the extended period, and this had to be completed by a certain date in order to be valid. It is this extension form that the IRS claimed was filed late by Mr. Flowers Co. and thus disqualified the plan.

The good news is the IRS agent was wrong.

The Mr. Flowers Co. 401(k) plan uses a fiscal year as their plan year as opposed to a calendar year. In reviewing this documentation with the XYZ Fund Company people, they explained that they believed the extension was filed timely given the fiscal year of the plan. We researched this further to find that the IRS actually issued their own revenue procedure notice, referred to as a "rev. proc.," specifically addressing fiscal year plans and noting that they had a longer period within which to file their extension form for the remedial amendment period given their plan year end date. As a result, we found that Mr. Flowers Co. did, in fact, file the extension form as well as all document updates on time. What the IRS agent failed to note was that this was a fiscal year plan, and there was a rev. proc. that allowed them until a full year following their plan year end in 2001 to file their remedial extension form. The form was filed in September 2002.

At that point, we were feeling good about ourselves. So the people from Mr. Flowers Co. and I drafted a letter in response to the IRS explaining all this and referencing the applicable rev. proc. to justify our position. We asked, in light of these facts and circumstances, that he drop his claim that the plan was disqualified and provide a written release accordingly. Shortly thereafter, we received a letter from the IRS agent, which vaguely reasoned that in spite of our claims, he did not agree that the rev. proc. in question applied to us. As a result, the extension was filed late, and he was going to uphold his decision that the plan was disqualified. He did kindly offer that Mr. Flowers Co. could participate in the "voluntary compliance resolution" (VCR) program, which is a fancy way of saying, "pay us money, and we'll let you off the hook." In short, Mr. Flowers Co. would have to pay a hefty fine.

While I will admit that I spoke to an ERISA attorney and double-checked my research, I knew we were right. The IRS agent was trying to bully Mr. Flowers Co. into paying a fine to get him off their back.

I advised Mr. Flowers Co. that they should hire the ERISA attorney and have him cite the rules in a letter to the IRS and demand that they release the issue. The ERISA lawyer was hired and did proceed to file a letter with the IRS citing the issues. There was no response from the IRS for more than six months. In spite of repeated efforts to contact the IRS agent, and several follow-up letters from the ERISA attorney, there was still no response.

Finally, almost a full year after the audit, the IRS wrote back to Mr. Flowers Co. and released the case, acknowledging that the extension form was in fact filed on time given the fiscal year of the plan. It was a hard-fought battle. If the IRS can cause all this over a supposed late filing of an extension form, can you imagine the level of pain inflicted upon the plan sponsor if there really is something wrong with their plan? The fact is there are hefty penalties for minor administrative oversights.

When a plan is found to be out of compliance with the tax law, a fine of $30,000 to $50,000 is commonplace. Larger penalties could be levied based on the significance of the noncompliance and the size of the plan. The degree to which you, the plan sponsor, raise the ire of our beloved governing organizations will have a lot to do with the type of penalty you may face. Factors affecting the size of sanctions levied are the degree to which harm may have been brought to plan participants, the deliberateness and/or awareness of the compliance failure, and whether or not efforts were made to correct a problem immediately upon discovery of said problem. However, one of the most egregious and severely penalized actions would be those that are intentionally designed to provide excess benefits to the owners of the company through the act of noncompliance. For this, you shall pay!

For these reasons, as well as an employer's obligations to their plan participants, it is now more important than ever to know the regulations that govern your plan and your responsibilities therein. I also believe that it is now more a necessity than a luxury to have a third party "named fiduciary" for your plan. You may choose to hire an ERISA attorney, but that can be expensive. The best positioned, and least expensive, choice for the job would be your investment advisor as long as they are qualified.

Employers and plan sponsors often ask me with a hint of disgust why so many burdens are placed on them simply to provide a benefit to their employees. I have a client named Scott who operates a machine shop with just over 100 employees. Scott has a very direct way of expressing himself, particularly if it's about something that could cost him money. We recently established a 401(k) plan for Scott's company. He previously maintained a SIMPLE IRA plan for his employees. However, the company outgrew that plan by rule, once their employee count went over 100. As I explained the various rules to Scott and his responsibilities as the employer, he became concerned to say the least. He wondered why he should have to pay a plan administrator to prepare plan documents as well as a CPA to come and audit his plan.

"Why should I pay for all this and put myself in a position of liability if something goes wrong? I'm doing this for my employees. I don't care about the plan myself. I already have plenty of money saved. I think I should just cancel the !@#king thing (retirement plan) and give out bonuses."

I responded to Scott by saying first that I agree, it is a significant responsibility to sponsor a retirement plan. Unfortunately, the ERISA and IRS rules are geared more to protect the employees than to reward the business owner for providing the benefits of a 401(k). Many rules have been developed as a result of employers discriminating against employees, failing to act as a fiduciary for the plan, or failing to send in employee payroll deductions in a timely manner. On the other hand, there are many benefits to you, the employer, to have a plan for your employees. These benefits include an ability to attract and retain good employees and provide incentive for them to perform well and build a career with your company—thus helping you build your business and grow your profits. A failure to offer any type of retirement plan in today's world may result in quality people leaving and going to work for your competitors.

Is it fair to say that the cost of replacing them and managing a revolving door of employees is far greater than the cost of maintaining your 401(k) plan?

The good news for Scott is that we set up his plan in a way to establish fiduciary excellence from the start. We suggested an array of very low cost investment alternatives so that the overall plan costs could be kept to a minimum, both for the employer and for the plan participants. We implemented a suite of services, including a named fiduciary to create an investment policy statement, recommend an investment lineup that meets the highest fiduciary standards, provide periodic monitoring of the plan investments and fees, provide participant communication and education, and provide general oversight of the compliance needs for the plan. The combination of these services, along with the standard plan administration and record keeping, significantly reduce Scott's liability as a plan sponsor. Needless to say, he doesn't swear at me anymore!

If you have a plan established directly through a single mutual fund company, *run* to the phone and call a qualified, registered investment advisor and ask them for a proposal of services and costs to be a named fiduciary for your plan. You may be pleasantly surprised to find that the net cost to upgrade is minor, if anything at all, yet the benefits to the plan sponsor and improvements for the participants are dramatic.

Many plan sponsors and/or their HR professionals believe that the mutual fund company or 401(k) plan vendor that they have the plan with acts as their fiduciary. They are completely mistaken.

The reasoning to engage a third party named fiduciary if you work directly with a mutual fund company is well justified. In the simplest of terms, it provides the ability to shift responsibility and potential liability away from your firm to a qualified professional. However, the benefits go much deeper. By using an independent registered investment advisor to manage your 401(k) plan, you can establish unbiased investment selection, investment fee benchmarking, and independent monitoring of your plan investments to assure you maintain a quality lineup. A single mutual fund company simply cannot offer a truly unbiased selection process for your plan investments. As a result, your fiduciary responsibility is not being met. Having an unbiased view of the universe of investment alternatives will lead to choices that help to keep costs down and improve performance over time for your plan participants. It's a clear win-win.

In the event of an audit by the IRS, they cannot find fault with your investment selection process, and meanwhile your employee appreciation level is improved. It starts with taking the steps that will meet your fiduciary responsibilities as a plan sponsor to conduct due diligence in your investment selection process.

IT'S A LEGAL OBLIGATION

In the absence of a qualified independent investment advisor, it may be difficult to comply with your fiduciary duties to plan for proper investment selection. Consider the alternative; you have a 401(k) plan with ABC Mutual Fund Co. There are 15 investment choices, 12 of which are ABC funds, and the other three were suggested by the plan service rep at the time you set up the plan. Here are some questions to ask yourself:

- Do you have reason to believe that all of the investment choices in your plan are among the best alternatives in their respective investment style group?

- Have the investment funds performed above average within their peer group?

- Do you have a mechanism to benchmark the fees associated with your investments to determine if they are at or below average?

- Has there been independent, unbiased investment monitoring performed regularly to document that the risk factors in the investments are appropriate for the stated investment style and that all of the appropriate investment styles are being covered in your offering?

It may be that, at the time you established the plan, the ABC service rep gave you a report about the funds that showed some of these things were true. However, if you have not been receiving regular, unbiased reports comparing your fund choices to the universe of their peers, if you have not acted on those reports and changed underperforming investments or high-cost investments to more optimal alternatives, you are failing in your fiduciary responsibility to the plan. In fact, if you've answered no to any of the previously noted questions, you are at risk for liability arising out of your fiduciary failures.

You have a legal obligation to conduct due diligence in your investment selection process. As a plan sponsor, in the absence of a third party designee, you are the ERISA fiduciary for the plan. An ERISA fiduciary is held to the highest standards of any fiduciary under the law. While a fiduciary, under the law, is held to the *prudent man rule*, an ERISA fiduciary is held to the *prudent expert rule*. Comparing these two is like comparing night and day! The prudent man rule would require a fiduciary to act in accordance with that which a prudent person would expect and/or judge to be in the best interest of a third party. The prudent expert rule is far less forgiving in that an ERISA fiduciary must act in accordance with that which an "expert" would be expected to do. I have yet to meet a business owner, HR specialist, or business manager who would be comfortable taking responsibility for being an "expert" in the same manner as an ERISA fiduciary.

Chances are, if you are working directly (without an independent advisor) with a single mutual fund company, you have answered no to one or more of the above questions. Let's take this a step further: many mutual fund companies will require that you offer the majority of choices in your plan using their proprietary funds. In return, they discount the record-keeping fees.

Does this quid-pro-quo minimum requirement compromise your fiduciary obligations and the quality of your investment choices? In case you need help, the answer is a resounding *yes*!

Is this a violation of ERISA sect. 408(b)(2)? Quite possibly, it is, particularly if the fees in the proprietary funds are higher than the industry average or performance is below average.

In plans where the majority of investment choices are from one mutual fund company, it's common to find that some number of them is below grade by ERISA due diligence standards.

As the plan sponsor, you have an obligation to assure that the fees charged to your plan and plan participants are "reasonable." Failure to conduct due diligence in this regard is a violation of ERISA Sect. 408(b)(2). Further, failure to offer low-cost alternatives such as index funds or ETFs may be construed as a breach of fiduciary responsibility. It is incumbent upon the plan sponsor to evaluate the costs and investment expenses in their plan through a valid benchmarking process to comply with the "reasonable fees" test.

In the first case of its kind to reach a court judgment, the Tibble v. Edison International case represents a landmark decision that affects plan sponsors everywhere. Essentially, this case is about 401(k) investment fees and the accusation by employees that the plan sponsor failed to offer lower cost versions of the investments in the plan. A district court found in favor of the employees, stating that it was a breach of fiduciary duty to offer retail shares rather than institutional share classes of certain mutual funds.

TIBBLE V. EDISON INTERNATIONAL: EXCESSIVE FEES FINALLY GO TO TRIAL

"On Aug. 9, 2010, the US District Court for the Central District of California in Tibble v. Edison International ("Tibble") entered the first judgment after trial in a so-called Employee Retirement Income Security Act "excessive fee" class action case. The judgment was entered after a three-day bench trial and following the court's earlier rulings on the parties' cross-motions for summary judgment. Despite the plethora of claims raised in the litigation seeking hundreds of millions of dollars in alleged damages to the plan related to fees, the only claim on which the plaintiffs prevailed was the single claim that the plan fiduciaries breached their fiduciary duty of prudence with regard to investments in the retail share classes—rather than the institutional share classes—of three mutual funds. The court awarded $370,732 in damages to the plan in connection with the claim, and further ordered defendants to replace the retail share class of one of the funds with the less expensive, but otherwise identical, institutional share class of the same fund."[4]

Other cases of this type have followed, and the settlements have been substantial, as larger plans have come under fire. The following are the headlines for recent cases against Bechtel Engineering and General Dynamics:

BECHTEL SETTLES 401(K) FEE CASE FOR $18.5M

Engineering giant Bechtel has agreed to an $18.5 million settlement of an excessive 401(k) fee suit.

"A Los Angeles Times news report said the agreement would end proceedings in a class action case filed by two former Bechtel employees in California who alleged the company violated its Employee Retirement Income

---

4 Reproduced with permission from Pension & Benefits, Reporter, 37 BPR 2349, 10/26/10, 10/26/2010. Copyright 2010 by The Bureau of National Affairs, Inc. (800-372-1033) http://www.bna.com For more information refer to the full article.

Security Act (ERISA) fiduciary responsibilities by not using its size to get lower fees from vendors."

PARTIES SETTLE GENERAL DYNAMICS 401(K) FEE CASE

General Dynamics Corporation and Fiduciary Asset Management (FAMCO) have agreed to a $15.1-million settlement of a 401(k) excessive fee lawsuit.

"A news release issued by the two defendants along with plaintiffs' law firm Schlichter, Bogard & Denton said insurance companies representing General Dynamics and FAMCO "and other sources" will pay the $15.1 million amount. The deal would dispose of the 2006 suit, Will, et al. v. General Dynamics Corp., et al., Case No. 06-698, that alleged the plan paid excessive fees and had committed other fiduciary breaches under the Employee Retirement Income Security Act (ERISA)."[5]

It's true that most small- to medium-size employers would not have as large a judgment against them as a Bechtel. However, these cases establish a legal precedent that is unmistakable. Plan sponsors have a fiduciary obligation to offer the lowest cost investment options that would be available to them given the size and nature of their plan. This means three things to the average small business owner.

First, you must conduct periodic fee benchmarking studies for your plan, particularly focusing on the investment expenses.

---

5 August 6, 2010 (PLANSPONSOR.com)

Second, you must seek to offer low-cost investment alternatives when available.

Third, you should have an independent advisor using recognized research systems to monitor the expenses and performance of your plan's investment options.

This advisor should be capable of offering an unbiased approach to choosing the best alternatives for your plan. A failure to establish and conduct these processes represents a failure to meet your fiduciary requirements as a plan sponsor. Thus, you would be exposed to liability arising out of said failure.

When you consider all of the complexity in the legislation surrounding 401(k) plans, and your exposure to potential sanctions resulting from plan audits, designing your plan to be compliant from the start is a good idea. A well-designed retirement plan must include a thorough service package that will provide the plan sponsor with independent, ongoing due diligence and oversight. This approach will lend itself to a simpler, more confident process for remaining in compliance and a higher degree of employee appreciation. If you're going to have to meet all the compliance requirements to provide benefits for your employees, wouldn't it be best to design the plan to impress them?

ACTION ITEM

Examine your retirement plans' service agreements, and identify all of the services available through your current providers. Use the following checklist to determine which additional services you should seek.

Services Checklist

Registered Investment Advisor

- Named fiduciary service

- Investment policy statement

- Investment selection guidance

- Periodic investment monitoring

- Fiduciary/trustee meetings (semi-annual)

- Fee benchmarking system

- Fee disclosure & ERISA 408(b)(2) compliance services

- Employee education meetings (quarterly option)

- Participant guidance

Third Party Administrator (TPA)

- Plan record keeping and reporting

- Compliance testing and IRS filings

- Employee communication materials and periodic statements

- Website access including retirement planning programs

- Retirement goal/needs assessment features

- ERISA 408(b)(2) fee disclosure services

Third Party Trustee & Custodial Services

- Oversight of plan assets, contributions, distributions, and loans

---

BUILDING A BETTER 401(K) PLAN

Building employee morale and loyalty through benefit plans is a meaningful objective that can bring great value to your organization. When you consider the importance of a retirement plan to a valued employee's financial future, it's easy to envision how a well-designed plan could be truly appreciated. The intangible benefits are lower turnover rates, more career-oriented people, employee buy-in to corporate goals, and new business initiatives, as well as employees willing to help improve profitability. Put simply, your 401(k) plan is about money, and people love it when their money has a good home.

The core of my philosophy for designing an optimal retirement plan benefit is that with a relatively small investment (as compared to other benefits such as health insurance) an employer can reap a great reward. Employee appreciation can be an illusive goal among employers and HR professionals. The value of successfully building employee morale through appreciation for benefit programs is priceless. Further, employers who take the time and due diligence to optimize their retirement plan will kill two birds with the proverbial stone. The more effectively you choose your service provider(s), the more successful you'll be in building a quality retirement plan that will give your employees reason to brag and simultaneously lowering your chances of being subjected to penalties for fiduciary shortcomings. For example, if you have a service provider who can reduce your investment expenses, you and your employees will save money year after year. By having lower investment costs, there's a good chance that your plan participants will have higher account balances over time given the same market performance. Larger account balances will mean better incomes for your employees when they reach their goal of financial independence. At the same time, this will be a step toward insulating your business from fiduciary failure under ERISA sect. 408(b)(2).

With the advent of ERISA sect. 408(b)(2), employees will now be receiving periodic reports illustrating the fees associated with their investments and any other charges attributed to them for participating in their 401(k) plan. Certainly it would be best for your employees to believe that their fees are reasonable as opposed to finding out they are excessive.

We recommend that employers avoid any packaged 401(k) products where there are significant limits on the number or array of investments. These packaged products, commonly offered through insurance companies and third party vendors, may also have hidden or excess fees. We strongly advise that you avoid products from vendors who impose requirements that you offer the majority of investment choices from their proprietary mutual funds. As a frame of reference, there are approximately 28,000 mutual funds and ETFs in the universe. Your plan should enable you to select an elite group of options from the universe with minimal limitation. It is also critically important that your plan choices include low-cost exchange traded and/or index funds as optional choices for your participants.

ACTION STRATEGY

Building a Better 401(k)/Retirement Plan

Review your plan provisions with the help of a specialist to assure that your plan is up to date with all current legislative changes and to offer the following:

- Roth 401(k) contribution option

- Contributions up to 90 percent of salary (subject to IRS maximum dollar amounts)

- In-service withdrawals as early as age 59½

- Vesting schedule of five years or fewer.

Establish an investment policy statement (IPS) to support your selection process, and review the list of available investments in your 401(k) plan and determine how many ETFs and/or low cost index mutual funds are available. The term "low cost" is intended to reference institutional class investment funds or funds with an expense ratio of .35 percent or lower. Many index funds and ETFs have an expense ratio of less than .2 percent. If your plan does not offer ETF investments or have more than a token low-cost index fund, you are advised to conduct such due diligence to consider additions to your investment offerings of that type.

Ask your advisor to provide regular investment monitoring reports that include alternative choices for those funds that may be underperforming or too expensive. These should be made available quarterly.

Review your employee communication policy. Make a plan to conduct at least two meetings per year where an investment professional will come to your offices and educate your participants on investment strategy, website usage, retirement planning, and plan specifications or benefits.

Offer matching benefits for your employees. Ask your third party administrator to provide an illustration of a proposed matching level based on your current plan participants. This can be based on a predetermined budget amount. Consider the cost of health insurance and how it's taken for granted. Then consider how an outlay a fraction of that size could be so appreciated by your employees that it improves their morale and possibly their work ethic and productivity.

Be sure to conduct periodic fee benchmarking to assure that your plan costs are reasonable and competitive in the marketplace. You would want your company to be viewed as competitive when attempting to hire quality employees. You should want your retirement plan to be competitive for the same reasons.

CHAPTER 9

ADVANCED TAX RULES AND PLAN FEATURES

Throughout the book, I've spoken of how Uncle Sam is offering you assistance to build your personal money machine through interest-free loans and tax-favored earnings. Well, Uncle Sam has some of his own stipulations in order for you to qualify for these benefits and to retain them into the future as part of your financial freedom plan.

In this chapter, we outline the rules of the game in terms of how to put money into a plan on a tax-favorable basis, the options you'll have to take money out, and the related tax consequences. Your objective should be to use these rules to maximize the tax benefits provided to you, understand how to build your financial freedom plan around your retirement plan, and minimize the taxation of your personal money machine profits.

Internal Revenue Code, Sect. 401(a) addresses tax rules relative to retirement plans. Subsection 401(k) provides the regulations relative to plan design guidelines, the federal tax treatment of contributions, and the associated limits, investment options, and types of withdrawals allowed for 401(k) plan participants. This section also addresses the taxation of distributions under the different withdrawal scenarios. This, of course, includes who can contribute, how money can be deposited, employer rules, contribution limits, and many, many other rules affecting your retirement savings opportunities, including the way your family can benefit from your 401(k) plan if you're no longer with us.

I'll break this chapter down into two general categories: "Contributions (Money In)" and "Withdrawals (Money Out)."

One of the first and most frequently asked questions I receive from 401(k) plan participants when they are considering investing in a 401(k) plan are:

"How can I get my money out when I need it?"

"What will the tax implications be when I begin to withdraw?"

While it's human nature to want the confidence of knowing how to hold onto what's yours, I think it's important to focus on building wealth first. Remember that obtaining a personal money machine is a great accomplishment. To be successful and achieve this accomplishment, you must make consistent payments on layaway. Like any other layaway plan, you cannot draw those payments back out prematurely, or you will defuse your opportunity to obtain that prize. So let's first understand how you may contribute to your 401(k) plan on a tax-advantaged basis to build substantial wealth, and then review the rules for withdrawing money in the future.

CONTRIBUTIONS—MONEY IN

There are only three ways for you to get money into a 401(k) plan.

The first way is having money deducted from your paycheck and deposited into the plan.

The second way is rolling over money from a prior employer's plan or other tax-qualified retirement plan (such as an IRA) into your current plan.

The third way is your employer making contributions on your behalf.

Your employer may have certain eligibility requirements (time and service) before you can participate in the retirement plan. For example, you may have to be employed for up to one year, during which you work a minimum of 1,000 hours (at 20 hours per week) to become eligible to join the plan. This would be the most restrictive eligibility requirement allowed by IRS regulations. Many employers have shorter periods of employment required, such as one to six months. When the period of employment required to become eligible to join is less than one year, there cannot be a minimum of hours worked required, so part-time employees are also likely to be eligible. If you are employed and not yet eligible to join a new employer's plan, you may still proceed to roll over money from a prior employer's plan into the new plan immediately. The eligibility requirement only applies to your ability to contribute from your salary and to receive employer contributions.

As an eligible participant in the plan, you may contribute up to *$18,000 per year* (as of 2015) out of your earnings. There is no longer an IRS limit on the percentage of your earnings that you may contribute, except that you may only contribute your gross earnings minus deductions for Social Security and Medicare; that nets out to approximately 92 percent. You may also have other deductions for things like health care and insurance. The IRS sets the dollar limit each year and may adjust it upward in increments of $500. For example, the dollar limit in 2011 was $16,500, 2012 was $17,000, and 2014 was $17,500.

Employees who are age 50 or older (including those who turn age 50 within a plan year) have the option to contribute up to an additional $6,000 per year as of 2015. This is called a *catch-up contribution* and is intended to assist those people who are closer to their desired financial freedom age and need to make up for shortfalls in their savings levels. Thus, a person age 50 can contribute a total of $24,000 as of 2015.

If you are a high wage earner, you may be classified as a "highly compensated employee" (HCE). The definition of an HCE is anyone earning over $120,000 a year as of 2015. If you are an HCE, you may have some limits on the percentage of your pay that can be contributed as a result of the discrimination rules set forth by the IRS. These rules essentially limit the average percentage contributions of the HCEs in a company based on the average of the "non-highly compensated employees" (NHCE). You will find out if you've contributed too much after the end of the plan year. If your company failed the average deferral percentage test, you may receive a refund of your excess contribution, which will be added back to your taxable income (for pretax contributions). If your employer offers a "safe harbor 401(k)," the above noted discrimination test will be waived, and all employees are free to maximize their contributions regardless of what other employee groups choose to do.

The table below illustrates the current benefit and compensation limits set forth by the IRS for qualified retirement plans:

Item	IRC Reference	2014 Limit	2015 Limit
401(k) and 403(b) Employee Deferral Limit	402(g)(1)	$17,500	$18,000
457 Employee Deferral Limit	457(e)(15)	$17,500	$18,000
Catch-up Contribution	414(v)(2)(B)(i)	$5,500	$6,000
Defined Contribution Dollar Limit	415(c)(1)(A)	$52,000	$53,000
Eligible Compensation Limit	401(a)(17); 404(l)	$260,000	$256,000
Highly Compensated Employee Income Limit	414(q)(1)(B)	$115,000	$120,000
Key Employee Officer	416(i)(1)(A)(i)	$170,000	$170,000
Social Security Taxable Wage Base		$117,000	$118,500

The limits above are with reference to defined contribution retirement plans such as 401(k)s and not with reference to defined benefit pension plans. Each limit is referenced by the applicable Internal Revenue Code section published by the IRS.
The dollar amounts listed above will change in future years based on IRS decisions relative to periodic cost of living adjustments. Highly compensated employees are defined based on their preceding year's earnings and whether they met that definition in that preceding year.

As you can see, the employee deferral limit is the same for 401(k), 403b (nonprofit), and 457 (government) retirement plans. The catch-up contribution is the additional deferral amount allowed for people age 50 and above. The "defined contribution dollar limit" refers to the total amount that can be deposited on your behalf from all contribution sources, your own and your employer's. This is the maximum amount you can contribute and/or receive based on the IRS limits in 2015. If you earned $100,000, contributed $24,000, and received a match of $4,000, you would be able to receive no more than $25,000 in profit sharing contributions from your employer. (If your employer is offering profit sharing contributions in the range of 25 percent of salary, please send me their name and address so I can apply for a job there!)

What makes qualified retirement plans like 401(k)s so attractive is that Uncle Sam provides us with a number of tax incentives to participate. As previously discussed, he will essentially extend you an interest-free loan and/or tax-free earnings on your savings for putting money into the plan and keeping it there until reaching your financial independence after age 59½. These tax benefits can be taken advantage of in two ways, the traditional method and the Roth 401(k) method.

LET'S MAKE A DEAL!

You have three choices in determining the tax treatment of your 401(k) contributions. You may have contributions deducted from your pay before tax (traditional 401(k) method), deducted from your paycheck after being taxed (a Roth 401(k) election), or a combination of the two.

Under the *traditional 401(k) method*, your payroll deductions come out before they are taxed (interest-free loan) thereby giving you a current tax savings and having those dollars deposited directly into your PRM layaway plan. The earnings on these contributions will be tax deferred, meaning that they will not be taxed until you withdraw them for income in later years. Thus, Uncle Sam is deferring the receipt of income tax on your contributions as well as your earnings on that money to help you save for your future. When you withdraw those funds after age 59½ you will have to pay tax on the distributions as ordinary income (see withdrawal rules).

Under the *Roth 401(k) method,* your contributions will be deducted from your paycheck after they've been taxed, there will be no current tax on the earnings (tax deferred), and you will be able to withdraw those contributions *and* all the investment earnings tax-free (tax exempt) after age 59½ (see withdrawal rules).

Thus with Roth, you're foregoing the interest-free loan on your contributions to have the advantage of not paying any taxes on the distributions during your financial freedom years.

Roth accounts also offer a number of unique tax advantages that may help you reduce or manage taxation of other income sources during your financial freedom years.

> Roth distributions do not count in the formula that determines the percentage of your Social Security benefits that will be taxed as ordinary income, 0 percent, 50 percent, or 85 percent.

> Income from Roth accounts will not impact how much you have to pay in Medicare Part B premiums. These costs generally go up the more income you have.

> Unlike traditional IRAs and 401(k)s, Roth accounts do not have required minimum distributions at age 70½. This may allow you to reduce your gross taxable income at that age.

Clearly, there are distinct advantages to each of the two contribution methods. The difficulty in deciding between the two may stem from the fact that while Roth account balances are more attractive to have when you're retired, the immediate tax savings from the traditional method makes it easier for you to meet your required savings levels. Keep in mind that you may also choose to have some of your contributions deducted pretax and some after tax.

So which is your best choice, door #1, door #2, or door #3?

I advise my clients that the first consideration is to be sure you are meeting your minimum PRM layaway amount (savings compensation), and use the tax savings to help you get there. While it will be valuable to have Roth assets, it is most important that you have sufficient assets. Once you can afford to contribute the necessary percentage of your salary with less up-front tax savings, begin to allocate some of your contributions to Roth, keeping in mind that you can mix the two in any ratio you choose. Increase the allocation to Roth vs. traditional over time while maintaining your appropriate savings compensation percentage.

Employer contributions come in two general types; matching and profit sharing. The term profit sharing is really a catchall for various employer contributions that are not based on matching employee contributions (nonelective contributions) and does not require that the employer actually take the money from profits or even have profits at all. All employer contributions are made pretax, meaning that they will go into your traditional 401(k) account without taxation to you and will be subject to income tax when they are withdrawn, including tax on earnings.

Matching contributions are the most popular form of employer contribution. They benefit employees by matching their payroll deductions with additional employer contributions based on a percentage of the employee's contribution. Usually employers will have an upside limit on the percentage of your salary that they are willing to match, such as 3 percent or 6 percent.

For example, an employer matching provision might state that the employer will provide a matching benefit of 50 percent of your contributions made up to the first 6 percent of your salary. In other words, if you have a salary of $50,000 and you contribute 6 percent ($3,000), your employer will add a matching benefit of $1,500 (or 50 percent of your contribution). However, because there is an upside limit on how much they will match, if you put in 10 percent of your salary ($5,000), you would still only get the same $1,500 (50 percent match on first 6 percent of salary contributed). For those people who don't contribute at least 6 percent of their salary, they will lose out on all or part of that benefit being offered. This gives rise to the importance of savings compensation. It's always wise to contribute at least as much as your employer will match.

Matching and profit sharing benefits are usually subject to a vesting schedule, which determines how much of that money will stay with you if you change jobs. Vesting refers to ownership in those benefits and is usually based on your years of service with the company. The most restrictive vesting schedule allowed would be a six-year graduated schedule under which you would earn 20 percent ownership in the employer contributions for each year of service with the employer after the first year in which you were hired. The main purpose of a vesting schedule is to give employees an incentive to stay with the company long term. *If you frequently switch employers, you may lose benefits.*

One of the reasons that so many employers have stopped providing pension plans is that defined benefit pension plans represent a financial commitment, and the employer is required to make the necessary contributions to fund a previously defined benefit for their employees regardless of how well their business is doing. This can be a problem during poor economic times or when business isn't doing well. It also presents challenges if investment returns aren't sufficient.

In our global economy, employers face competition from around the world. Most foreign corporations do not have the cost of providing pensions, which are an expensive employee benefit. Thus, their products can be made and sold for less.

With 401(k) plans, employer contributions are most often discretionary, unless they have made an advanced commitment to do so, such as in "safe harbor" plans. The term *discretionary* means that your employer is not under any obligation to contribute to your account but makes contributions in an effort to benefit their employees. Consider the term profit sharing; it stems from the principal that your employer would want to have their valued employees share in the profits of the company. Obviously, this would have to allow the employer to look back after the end of a given year and see what type of profits and/or growth they achieved before determining if such a benefit was affordable. This also provides employers with the opportunity to determine the right amount of such contributions given all the surrounding circumstances. Thus, profit sharing contributions are discretionary. Traditional matching benefits are also discretionary in that they can be changed by your employer at any time by providing advance notice to participants of the change.

Safe harbor 401(k) plans offer attractive benefits to employees as well as to the small employer. Generally, safe harbor plans are elected by employers of less than 100 employees. However, there is no rule of eligibility based on employee count. Under a safe harbor plan, the employer makes a decision at the beginning of each year to commit to a minimum matching formula or a minimum nonelective contribution benefit (similar to a profit sharing contribution). Once the plan year commences, these contributions are required for that year and cannot be withheld at the discretion of the employer. The employer may stop these contributions in future years should they find that it's unaffordable. The safe harbor plan can be attractive to small employers, as it eliminates the need for certain discrimination tests that may limit contributions by the highly compensated employees (including owners). The IRS essentially is saying that if an employer will commit to provide a minimum benefit (of 3 to 4 percent of salary) to their employees, the highly compensated employees in the company will have the freedom to maximize their own contributions to the plan.

The safe harbor matching election requires the employer to match 100 percent of your contributions up to the first 3 percent of your salary and 50 percent of the next 2 percent of your salary contributed or a total of a 4 percent match. As with all matching benefits, if you don't contribute enough, you may miss out on all or part of that benefit. A safe harbor nonelective contribution requires the employer to contribute 3 percent of salary to all eligible employees regardless of their contribution levels. Safe harbor contributions are always fully vested immediately once deposited in the employee's account.

ACTION ITEMS

Review your plan to determine the type of employer contributions you may have available to you as a participant and your current savings (payroll deduction) amount. If your employer offers a matching contribution, be sure that you are contributing enough to receive the full matching benefit.

Review your savings compensation requirement to satisfy your layaway plan. Deduct your employer contributions (as a percentage of your salary) and determine what percentage of your salary is needed to fulfill your needs to achieve your PRM. Adjust accordingly.

GETTING YOUR MONEY OUT

Your 401(k) plan account may already be the largest financial asset you have. Other than your home, it will likely become your most valuable asset, period. It may be tempting to tap into those assets from time to time as financial obligations present themselves. It is in those circumstances that you must remain confident in the knowledge of how your financial plan will work for you and what could cause it to fail. Remember the basic rule: Never take withdrawals. This implies that, in a true emergency, you may need to access some of this money. However, outside of a disability, your house burning down, or the need to pay off the mob or face certain death, you shouldn't use it for anything other than acquiring your Personal

Retirement Machine. If you must access your retirement assets prematurely, use the loan option, as this allows you to avoid current taxation and put the money back into your PRM layaway plan over time.

LOANS

Regarding withdrawals during your working years, there are a set of rules that will affect the way in which you can access funds and the potential tax implications. The first option is to take a loan. Virtually every 401(k) plan has a provision for loans by participants. However, loan provisions are not required, and the plan sponsor has the discretion to limit the number of loans or the circumstances under which a loan would be allowed. It is very rare that a 401(k) plan is established without some form of a loan provision. When I first started working with 401(k) plans in the 1980s, most plans restricted employees to taking loans for only four purposes: the purchase of a residence, to prevent eviction from or repair a residence, to pay college tuition, or to pay excess medical bills. These were called hardship provisions. Today it is more likely that your 401(k) plan will allow you to take a loan for any reason. Loans are allowed for up to 50 percent of your vested account balance and a maximum of $50,000 (whichever is less). Generally loans must be paid back in five years. In the case of the purchase of a primary residence, a ten-year amortization period is allowed. Loans must be paid back through payroll deduction. If you leave your current employment, a lump sum payment would be required to cover the unpaid balance or that balance would be taxed the same as an early withdrawal.

What's attractive about loans is that they are not subject to taxation so long as you pay them back. The interest you pay on the loan is credited back to your own account. With regular loan payments, you will be able to replenish your PRM layaway plan over time in spite of raiding those sacred funds. What's unattractive about loans is that employees often reduce their savings amount by the amount of the loan payment, which is a bad idea. Consider that you might be forever losing matching benefits while this happens and how that will negatively impact your chances of achieving your goal of financial freedom.

Another problem with loans is that the money you receive is actually withdrawn from your investment accounts. Therefore, it will not earn the returns that the markets have to offer until it's put back. Remember Aunt Gladys's story—she put the money in, never tried to time the market, never took a loan or a withdrawal, and $2,000 grew to nearly $100,000 in approximately 30 years.

HARDSHIP WITHDRAWALS

In order to take a withdrawal from your 401(k) while still employed, you must qualify for a hardship distribution. To qualify for a hardship distribution, you must either have a medical hardship (such as a disability) or need the funds to purchase a primary residence, pay for college tuition, or prevent eviction from a primary residence. Unlike loans, hardship withdrawals are fully taxable and will be subject to an early withdrawal penalty of 10 percent if you're under age 59½. There is one exception to the 10 percent penalty. The exception is for a *medical hardship*. In this case, ordinary taxation only would apply.

The problem with withdrawals is that *once you pay the tax, you can never get it back*. Not only that, once you withdraw money from your PRM layaway plan, you may not be able to put it back. The basic tax rule for withdrawals from traditional 401(k) assets is that, at the time they are taken, you will pay tax on the amount withdrawn as ordinary income. If you are under age 59½, you will also have to pay an additional 10 percent penalty on the amount withdrawn. This same tax treatment also applies to traditional IRA assets. *Taking an early withdrawal from your 401(k) plan or IRA is like paying Uncle Sam's interest-free loan back early.*

ROTH 401(K) DISTRIBUTIONS

For Roth 401(k) and Roth IRA assets, the withdrawal rules are slightly more complex. In Roth 401(k) and Roth IRA accounts, you are afforded tax-free distributions of all principal and earnings when distributed after a minimum five-year holding period *and* your attainment of age 59½. Withdrawals from a Roth account prior to age 59½ or prior to a five-year hold, whichever comes latest, will result in taxation of the earnings portion and a 10 percent penalty on those earnings if you're under 59½ years old. This represents a devastating financial blow. These are assets that will be tax exempt if held for five years and to age 59½. Tax exempt would indicate that you would never have to pay tax on them. They also provide several other valuable tax saving benefits and can be an invaluable component of your distribution plan during your financial freedom.

The five-year holding rule states that, *from the first day of the calendar year in which you make your first Roth deposit, you must wait five full calendar years before taking a withdrawal.* You must also attain the age of 59½ to qualify for the tax exemption. Even if you are over age 59½ when you take a withdrawal from a Roth account, if you violate the five-year rule, you will lose the tax exemption and be subject to ordinary income tax on the earnings. In other words, if you start your first Roth account at age 57, you cannot withdraw from it until age 62. If you first start contributing to a Roth account at age 50, you cannot withdraw from it until age 59½. Due to the complexity of these rules, most 401(k) plans do not allow Roth assets to be available for loans or hardship withdrawals in fear that an oversight of this rule could result in severe tax consequences.

The following is a simple outline of how distributions from Roth accounts would be taxed dependent on when they are withdrawn:

You are under age 59½, and you have not met the five-year rule for your Roth contributions:

You will be subject to ordinary income taxes and a 10 percent penalty on the earnings that are withdrawn.

You are over age 59½, but you have not yet met the five-year rule:

You will be subject to ordinary income tax on the earnings, but no penalty shall apply.

You have met the five-year rule, but you have not yet reached the age of 59½:

You will be subject to both ordinary income tax and a 10 percent penalty on the earnings withdrawn. Please see below for a list of exceptions to the 10 percent penalty.

You are over age 59½ and have met the five-year rule for Roth contributions:

Your withdrawals will be exempt from taxation.

You may avoid the 10 percent penalty noted above under any of the following circumstances:

1. You have unreimbursed medical expenses that exceed 7.5 percent of your adjusted gross income.

2. You are paying medical insurance premiums after losing your job.

3. The distributions are not more than your qualified higher education expenses.

4. The distribution is due to an IRS levy of the qualified plan.

5. The distribution is a qualified reservist distribution.

6. The distribution is a qualified disaster recovery assistance distribution.

7. The distribution is a qualified recovery assistance distribution.[6]

It seems that the feds want you to succeed in obtaining your own PRM so much that they've taken steps to discourage you from making mistakes such as taking withdrawals from your layaway plan prior to achieving financial freedom. That would be unthinkable! It may be that Uncle Sam knows something about the strength of the Social Security system or the lack thereof.

PENSION VS. 401(K)

I find it interesting that people lament over the fact that their parents had pensions, and they don't. I agree that the benefits afforded by pension plans are quite valuable. However, there are a number of

---

6 Source: IRS Publication 590

differences between pensions and 401(k)s that may be worth noting. Pension plans do not ever allow loans under any circumstances. Pension plans do not allow withdrawals until you work for 20 or 30 years for the same company and then elect your retirement benefits. The Bureau of Labor Statistics reported that the average employee tenure among wage and salary employees in 2012 was 4.6 years. They also found that less than 30 percent of the workforce had been with the same employer for more than ten years. It seems as though the average employee changes jobs approximately once every five years.

Even if you do retire with a pension, that plan will provide you with a fixed monthly income. Generally, that income amount never increases, and you will not have an option to take out additional lump sums to buy a boat or a vacation home. Maybe part of the reason pension plans are able to pay out such good benefits is that participants cannot touch the money while they're employed, nor can they take excess withdrawals during their retirement.

The reality is that one of the reasons pension plans are becoming obsolete is that we live in a "here and now" society. Most employees want to see the money in their paychecks each week, as opposed to a statement of future benefits. Employers must account for the costs to meet pension obligations down the road. Those are significant costs, and employers must generate revenue to cover those costs by raising prices for their goods and services or reducing current wages paid to employees. Higher prices will mean that your company may not be competitive in the marketplace. This will eventually lead to lost business and a loss of market share. When this happens, employers must lay off employees. Therefore, pension plan benefits must be accounted for by a reduction in current wages available to employees.

ROLLOVERS

Participants in virtually all tax-qualified retirement plans such as 401(k), 403(b), 457, SEPs, and SIMPLE plans are allowed to roll over their funds from those plans to another employer's qualified plan or to an IRA in the event they change employers, lose their job, or retire. They may also choose to roll over funds from an IRA into an employer-sponsored plan in many cases. When rollovers are administered properly, there is no tax consequence. There is simply a transfer of the assets from one type of qualified plan to another. Generally, the subsequent distribution rules will also stay the same. The only major exception to that statement would be when someone chooses to convert their IRA to a Roth IRA.

When a person converts a traditional IRA to a Roth IRA, they are required to pay the tax on the converted amount as if it were a withdrawal, except that there is no penalty for doing this at any age. While there are income limits for individuals to start and/or contribute to a Roth IRA, anyone can qualify to convert a traditional IRA to a Roth so long as they pay the applicable taxes. The decision to do such a conversion should be based on sound financial planning, as there are many factors that determine if the Roth conversion will be advantageous or not. Seek the advice of a qualified financial advisor to determine if a Roth conversion is something you should consider.

Traditional rollovers from a 401(k) plan to an IRA are done for very good reasons when a person enters into financial freedom. There are many advantages to having your PRM assets in an IRA over a 401(k) when you reach that stage in your financial life. In order to conduct a qualified rollover from an employer-sponsored ERISA retirement plan such as a 401(k) to an IRA, there are several important rules that must be followed in order to avoid a tax consequence. Ideally, when rolling your money from a 401(k) to an IRA, you want to have a direct rollover of the assets. A failure to abide strictly by the direct rollover rules can nullify the qualification of the rollover and result in significant tax consequences.

The essence of the direct rollover rules is that you cannot ever take receipt of the funds that are coming out of your 401(k) during the rollover process. So to comply, you or your financial advisor would create an IRA account (if you don't already have one) and simply arrange to have your check sent directly to the custodian of your IRA account. This is also referred to as a trustee-to-trustee transfer. There are no tax consequences in this type of transfer. Often a 401(k) plan will not send the check directly to another custodian and by rule will only send distribution or rollover checks directly to the participant. In those cases, the check will be sent to you and must be made payable to the custodian of your IRA, FBO (for benefit of) your name. When you receive the check, you must forward that check to your IRA custodian or your financial advisor for deposit directly into your IRA. *Do not* cash this check, as that would represent constructive receipt of the money and result in taxation of the amount as a distribution.

IRAs offer a variety of advantages over 401(k)s when you reach the point of financial freedom. An IRA can offer simplicity in terms of accessing your money. Whereas the IRS requires that all distributions from a 401(k) be subject to a 20 percent tax withholding (when you take out $10,000, you receive only $8,000), an IRA allows you to withdraw funds without any withholding and either pay them back to your IRA account within 60 days and avoid taxation or keep the money and pay tax on it when due. The IRA also allows an account holder to take income from their tax-qualified funds prior to age 59½ without the 10 percent penalty under rule 72T of the Internal

Revenue Code. This rule states that an IRA account holder may begin distributions from an IRA as early as age 55 without penalty so long as they receive a "series of substantially equal payments" based on their life expectancy.

I believe that there are two key advantages to an IRA over your employer-sponsored 401(k) or 403b.

- The IRA will offer you a much wider array of investment options than a 401(k) plan.

- The IRA also will offer you the capability to establish more complex beneficiary arrangements than typically allowed in 401(k) plans, which can be very favorable in your estate planning.

Employer-sponsored 401(k) and 403b plans typically have a finite list of investment options. While this list may be quite good for growth investing during your accumulation years, it may leave much to be desired during your distribution years. That's when reliability of income and preservation of capital become more prominent elements of your investment strategy. As we will discuss, your distribution strategy becomes paramount to your success during financial freedom. An IRA will give you the freedom to invest in the full universe of investment options, including annuities and other instruments that may offer certain guarantees to protect your income stream throughout your life. This will enable you to diversify your investment strategy to accomplish a wider range of needs.

Estate planning, like life insurance, has one primary objective: to care for your family and loved ones. In the case of estate planning, we look to organize your financial affairs to avoid waste or adverse tax consequence as well as to maintain family harmony after your passing. When it comes to qualified retirement plan assets, tax planning after death is often as important as tax planning during life. One of the great advantages of an IRA is that you may name as many beneficiaries and contingent beneficiaries as you wish, including children, grandchildren, and the "per stirpes" designation allowing for beneficiaries who have yet to be born. The reason this becomes an advantage is that your IRA can be stretched to benefit many people and to continue to defer taxes on the lump sum assets (subject to required minimum distributions) for many years after you die. Your estate can decide which of the listed beneficiaries it wishes to benefit up to nine months after you die. The younger the beneficiary, the more gradually they may take distributions from the IRA assets, thus deferring taxation for many, many years.

REQUIRED MINIMUM DISTRIBUTIONS

With all the tax benefits that Uncle Sam has given us in the 401(k) plan and in other retirement plans, there comes a time when payback is in order. That's what the feds mean by establishing the required minimum distribution (RMD) rules. Essentially that interest-free loan that Uncle Sam gave you will come due when you reach age 70½, and you must start to withdraw funds from your qualified retirement accounts either that year or no later than April 1 of the year following the year in which you turn age 70½. Yes, of course you will have to pay taxes on those withdrawals as well. As we know, Roth 401(k)s and Roth IRAs are not subject to RMDs, nor are they subject to taxation on distributions.

The amount you must withdraw is based on the "uniform lifetime table" of life expectancy factors. This table is established by the IRS. For each year older that you become, you will be required to take a higher percentage of your assets as your RMD. For example, in the year you turn 70½, you must withdraw 1/27.4 of your assets or 3.65 percent of the value of your qualified retirement accounts. This percentage goes up each year as your life expectancy in years goes down. The required withdrawal percentage will never be high enough to force you to withdraw all of your assets, however. For example, at age 75 you must withdraw 4.05 percent. The year you turn 85 you must withdraw 6.75 percent.

The RMD you must withdraw is based on the total value of your combined qualified retirement plans as of the end of the preceding year. Given that you are allowed to have multiple IRAs, you may take the percentage required from each one similarly or you may take it all from one IRA and leave others to grow or accumulate earnings without withdrawal. There are a number of reasons why you would be advised to have multiple IRAs, especially if you have company stock in your 401(k) plan (this should be held in an IRA account separate from all other IRA assets). A simple example would be the use of annuities as an investment or as a guaranteed income vehicle. This investment may stand alone in an IRA while you maintain a more traditional investment portfolio in another IRA. The income from the annuity may be enough to cover the full RMD requirement. Therefore, you would not need to draw from the portfolio if you didn't need income from that taxable source. There are many financial planning considerations when it comes to establishing IRA accounts and from which one you should draw income. Having a qualified financial advisor becomes even more important at this juncture, as mistakes can be quite costly.

DEATH OF A 401(K) PARTICIPANT

When a person dies, their financial assets become the subject of estate settlement rules and tax rules relative to the income taxable portion of their assets. This includes their 401(k) and other qualified retirement accounts. In essence, the balances of their 401(k) or IRA (exclusive of Roth accounts) become taxable unless they are rolled over to another tax-qualified account through the beneficiary designations of the deceased. If you have the unfortunate circumstance under which you die before finishing your working career, there will be options and obligations for your surviving spouse or heirs to consider relative to your 401(k) balance. These choices will also affect future withdrawal requirements and must be made carefully.

The simplest of cases is when a married person dies and leaves his or her spouse with a 401(k) account balance. The surviving spouse first has three fundamental choices:

- Take all or some of the money out of the 401(k) and pay the tax on the entire amount withdrawn.

- Roll the (remaining) account balance into an IRA in their own name.

- Maintain the account as a deceased spouse account either in the 401(k) or rolled into an IRA under that account title.

The most commonly advisable choice is for the surviving spouse is option 2; roll the account into an IRA under their own name. The IRS allows a surviving spouse the option of simply inheriting the qualified retirement account and retitling it in their own name. Then at their option they may roll it into an IRA. The significance of this choice is that there are no taxes payable as a result of the transfer. The surviving spouse has absolute ownership and control, and the required minimum distributions will be based on the age of the surviving spouse, as opposed to the deceased. In addition, the surviving spouse may name anyone they wish as beneficiary.

A spouse may elect to convert the deceased account into an inherited account or a "deceased spouse account." The reason this could be advisable is that it would allow a younger spouse to have access to RMD distributions without penalty prior to their reaching age 59½ should he or she have an income need.

Regardless of when a person dies, the tax rules for the balances in their tax-qualified retirement accounts will be roughly the same. Given that the tax rules relative to the treatment of a deceased person's IRA account are much the same as with their 401(k) or 403b, it is wise to consider the importance of proper beneficiary planning for all tax-qualified accounts. This may be part of an overall estate plan or may simply be part of a financial planning strategy to pass tax-advantaged assets to loved ones in the most advantageous way. While we don't want to have to think about it much, death is inevitable, and financial planning for that eventuality is as important to your family as financial planning is to you during your life.

ACTION ITEMS

Take the time to review your beneficiaries on your 401(k) account as well as all other qualified retirement accounts. Keep in mind that it is unwise to believe that investment houses or other retirement account vendors will keep proper records of your beneficiary designations. You must maintain adequate, up-to-date records to protect the interests of your heirs.

There are numerous tax implications relative to your beneficiary designations. A failure to establish an effective set of beneficiary designations may result in an accelerated taxation of your 401(k) or IRA account assets after your death or a lack of access to those assets by those people you truly wish to benefit.

Consider adding contingent beneficiaries to your 401(k), IRA, and all other tax-advantaged retirement accounts. Seek the opportunity to add "per stirpes" designations to your IRA beneficiary designations to benefit your children's children, for example. Consult a financial planner that can offer advice in the area of estate planning as well as the tax rules affecting a deceased's 401(k) or IRA account.

CHAPTER 10

RETIREMENT INCOME DISTRIBUTION STRATEGIES

Achieving financial freedom is a great accomplishment. To declare financial independence is to reach the top of the mountain, look down at the world from that peak, and know that you have succeeded. You will be among those who have achieved great things. It's akin to the feelings our forefathers had when they won the Revolutionary War and declared their independence from Great Britain. For everyone who reaches this point in their financial life, pride and jubilation will fill their soul in knowing that they are truly independent. So once you've gotten this far, it's important to understand how to manage your finances efficiently and assure that your dream of having a Personal Retirement Machine that can provide income for your lifetime is realized.

Understanding the distinction between your preferred investment style during your accumulation years and prudent investment strategies for your distribution years is a fundamental necessity in developing the optimal long-term PRM strategy. While you are working and saving money in your layaway plan, your investment strategy should be based on planning for the future and seeking growth opportunities for your assets so that you can achieve your goal. This period of your financial life is referred to as your *accumulation years*. Once you declare financial independence, you are no longer investing for the future; instead, you're investing to produce income now and for the rest of your life. This new period in your financial life is referred to as your *distribution years*. There are many fundamental differences in your investment strategy for these two scenarios, the biggest of which is that you are no longer adding new investment money to your portfolio during your distribution years. Another very big difference is that you'll begin drawing out income from these assets on a regular basis.

The way you manage money during your distribution years is likely very different from the way you might during your accumulation years.

One of the main objectives in your investment strategy during your distribution years will be to establish reliability of income (ROI) through the various investments you hold. The ROI on your investments and your risk of loss (allocation to stocks and other risk classes) will determine the stability of your PRM in rocky markets or poor economies. Your ability to weather a storm in the markets and maintain your income levels without selling into losses may determine the degree of success you will have in receiving income throughout your entire life. These factors will drive your investment decisions to stabilize your portfolio and your income during your financial freedom years. Finding investments that have both a high

ROI and a strong yield (5–6 percent) is not always easy, and you may have to sacrifice some portfolio features in order to find those investment alternatives that will accomplish this objective.

Therefore, there are two primary categories of distribution strategy that warrant careful planning; distribution order and ROI. One of the fundamental rules in developing any investment strategy is that you must understand your time horizon for the money you wish to invest before choosing which investment alternative will best suit your needs. During your distribution years, there is a greater need to maintain liquid assets, as you will need to draw funds regularly and you don't want to be forced to sell securities at a loss in down markets. Therefore, we must develop our distribution order first so that we will know how to invest different pools of assets. These different pools of assets could be managed for different purposes, such as current income and long-term growth. One way I describe this to my clients is to break the asset groups up into three or more "buckets" that correlate both distribution order and investment style. For example, let's say we establish a basic three-bucket strategy— a short-term liquidity bucket, an income bucket, and a long-term growth bucket.

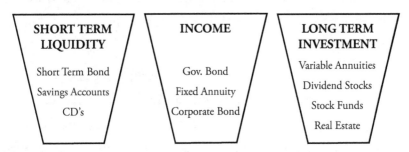

SHORT TERM LIQUIDITY

Short Term Bond
Savings Accounts
CD's

INCOME

Gov. Bond
Fixed Annuity
Corporate Bond

LONG TERM INVESTMENT

Variable Annuities
Dividend Stocks
Stock Funds
Real Estate

This example shows the three-bucket strategy and a sampling of the typical investment alternatives that would be appropriate for each bucket. This is in concert with the fact that we would initially draw the heaviest amount of annual income from left to right.

The bucket that is established as the primary income source in the short term has the shortest investment time horizon. Therefore, it must be invested most conservatively.

The third and largest bucket will be invested for the long haul. While this bucket may produce some income today, it is also responsible for providing us with our best options for positive long-term growth to provide income in later years. Because the assets in the third bucket are intended to provide income many years into the future, we will need investment returns to be well in excess of the inflation rate over that time period. This objective is typically associated with stock investing.

One of the fundamental benefits of establishing a bucket strategy is that *it helps to determine how much of our PRM assets should be allocated to each bucket and thus each investment type.* Using presumed average returns, we can calculate how much should be allocated to each bucket and estimate the number of years that bucket will continue to produce income. It is likely that our bucket strategy will call for you to exhaust most or all of the funds in the first and second bucket over a planned period of time while allowing the third bucket to grow larger.

These buckets can be made up of more than one account. They may incorporate IRA assets as well as after-tax savings accounts, although we typically would allocate a heavier weighting of IRA assets to the longer-term buckets. Keep in mind that there may be reasons to have more than one IRA account, such as managing your required minimum distributions, Roth IRAs, having different beneficiaries, or using annuities as an IRA investment.

We may take income from all three buckets simultaneously, being careful to plan how much we want from each bucket based on the level of taxation on that income or the income-producing capability of the investment holdings. The common purpose of a fourth bucket would have to do with a plan to leave an inheritance, leave money to a charity, or transfer funds to a trust. Once we establish a bucket strategy, we can move on to creating the appropriate distribution order.

The first step in the process of creating a distribution order is to understand which assets are most valuable and at what point in time it's best to use them. Some people would say, how can one dollar be more valuable than another? The answer is simple—taxation. One of the primary concerns with planning your financial independence is to determine the taxation of your distributions. Managing the tax treatment of your income in retirement is paramount to maximizing the assets you have and the Social Security benefits you will receive. It is also important to your heirs, as certain investments are going to be less favorable to leave behind than others. The objective in distribution planning is to keep the taxation of your income to a minimum as well as effectively managing your overall portfolio performance for net after-tax returns. A secondary consideration may be for the potential taxation of assets that you pass to your heirs after death.

There are four general types of taxable income you may receive during your financial freedom years:

- Ordinary income (taxed at the same rate as earned income)
- Interest income
- Capital gains
- Dividends

These various types of income are taxed differently by the feds and will also vary depending on which state you live in. At the federal level, interest is taxed as ordinary income while dividends are taxed at the same rate as long-term capital gains (as of 2013). For most people, the tax rate for long-term capital gains (15 percent in 2013) is lower than their marginal, ordinary income tax rate. However, state income taxes on interest income, dividends, and capital gains will vary widely. Obviously, if one type of income is taxed less than another source of income, the income that is taxed less is more valuable.

For example, dividend income can be more valuable than ordinary income, given that ordinary income is usually taxed at a higher rate. Therefore, having dividend-producing stocks in an ordinary (non-tax-qualified) account can be advantageous in producing income taxed at a low rate. Unfortunately, distributions from traditional IRAs and qualified retirement plans are always taxed as ordinary income regardless of the underlying securities or the type of income sources within the retirement account.

Excluding most gifts, trust fund distributions, and inheritances, there are also four types of tax-free income you may receive

- Roth IRA or Roth 401(k) distributions
- Municipal bond interest
- Distributions of principal from non-qualified savings
- Loans from life insurance cash value

For the purposes of this example, I will consider life insurance loans to be the same as withdrawals of principal from a nonqualified account.

Municipal bond interest is tax exempt at the federal level and may or may not be tax exempt in your home state. However, only two of these tax-free income sources are truly tax free to people who are receiving Social Security benefits: Roth distributions, and distributions of principal from non-qualified savings (including life insurance cash values subject to IRS limits).

Great care is warranted to draw the right mix of income from the various sources you have available to you in order to manage your overall taxation. Lower tax rates will result in higher net after-tax returns and more income generated from your PRM assets. This is largely due to the way in which the IRS taxes Social Security benefits. Social Security benefits are subject to income tax to a larger or smaller degree based on the amount of other income a person or couple may have. With higher levels of income, a higher percentage of your Social Security benefits will be subject to tax as ordinary income. The objective is to keep the taxable amount of Social Security benefits at 0 percent to 50 percent for as many years as possible. To calculate the taxation range you may be in, consider the following guidelines:[7]

> First, determine your total income other than Social Security and call this your "other income." This number should include all types of income regardless of source. Keep in mind that although municipal bond interest is tax exempt, the federal government requires that you count that as income for the purpose of determining your taxable Social Security benefit percentage. (You may exclude loans from life insurance from this calculation. However, note that life insurance loans could trigger a taxable event, and you should consult your tax advisor if this is an income that you are receiving.)
>
> Second, reduce your "other income" by withdrawals of principal from after-tax accounts. Also reduce your

---

7 Source: US Social Security Administration

"other income" by withdrawals from Roth accounts. This will leave you with your net "other income" that's attributable to your taxation rate on Social Security benefits.

Add one half of your total annual Social Security benefits (combined husband and wife) to your "other income" to determine your "base income." Your base income range will determine what percentage of your Social Security benefits will be subject to income tax as ordinary income.

Then compare this total to the base income ranges for your filing status. If your total is greater than the allowable base income range, that percentage of your benefits will be taxable.

The amount of your Social Security benefits that are subject to income taxation as of 2012:

Base Income Range	Married Filing Jointly	Single or Head of Household	Married Filing Separately
$0 - $25000	0%	0%	50%
$25,000 - $34,000	-	50%	85%
$34,000 & up	-	85%	85%
$32,000 - $44,000	50%	-	-
$44,000 & up	85%	-	-

Source: US Social Security Administration

As illustrated in Figure SS, once your base income crosses a threshold to a higher range, a higher percentage of your Social Security income will be subject to income tax. Therefore, it is wise to integrate non-attributable tax-free income from Roth accounts or savings principal into your distributions to avoid crossing the first or second threshold while still receiving the same amount of spendable cash. As you might see, there is real value in having sources for this type of income. For this reason, we urge 401(k) participants to attribute at least a portion of their 401(k) contributions to Roth. *If you can make significant contributions to Roth 401(k) on a consistent basis, you will be rewarded during your distribution years.*

When you consider that you must add half of your Social Security income to the other income total for this determination, it's reasonable to assume that most people will pay income tax on their SS benefits. However, with proper planning, there can be years when you pay less than in others or years when you pay no tax on those benefits. The longer you can extend that scenario, the more after-tax income you will keep. Further, when you can afford to use less of your nest egg during years when you pay less in taxes, you can leave more of your PRM assets to earn higher tax-favored returns to build and substantiate your future income.

The following is an example of a real life case for one of my clients who recently retired. His real name is Harry, but we will give him a different last name to protect his privacy. We'll call him Harry Safensound.

When Harry declared financial independence, he had a variety of income sources. Harry had a total financial freedom income need of $120,000 (before tax), and he expected to receive $30,000 of that need from Social Security. He declared financial independence at age 66 and established his PRM with just under $1,595,000. You may recall from chapter 6 that, in order for Harry to receive an income of $90,000 from his PRM, he needs to have $1.8 million (20 x $90,000) so that he could begin with a drawdown rate of 5 percent and have an inflation-adjusted income stream for 30 years. So when Harry made his decision, we knew that there was a shortfall. However, Harry had two things in his favor.

First, he waited until age 66 to begin. Second, he had approximately $250,000 in after-tax savings ($175,000 in the bank and $75,000 in Roth IRAs) that would not be taxed upon receipt as income. Harry is married and files a joint federal tax return with his wife, Matilda.

The key to maximizing the income producing capacity of Harry and Matilda's PRM is in the distribution order. Currently, at age 66, Harry and Matilda did not have any required minimum distributions for the next five years.[8] Given that the Safensounds would be able to receive a significant portion of their income free of tax, we can design a mix of distribution sources to keep tax rates low, and minimize the taxation of Social Security benefits. This is done by taking income from those sources that don't count toward the calculation of taxable Social Security benefits. During the initial years of financial independence, we were able to reduce the gross amount needed of $120,000 by the tax savings from using our strategy (using after-tax savings first). We estimated that in the years that Harry and Matilda only took $15,000 per year from taxable sources, and they had less than $2,000 per year in interest earnings from the bank, they would have no tax liability on their Social Security income. Therefore, in those years their tax liability would be based only on the $15,000 they withdrew from their IRA and any interest they earned at the bank. The remainder of their income needs would be drawn from the bank savings first and then from the Roth IRA. While tax rates may vary based on residency and potential deductions, we determined a reasonable assumption of tax on an income of $120,000 would be $25,000 while the tax on only $15,000 of income would be near zero. I base this on Harry and Matilda having approximately $20,000 of personal or itemized deductions and a 25 percent blended tax rate on the balance.

8 RMDs must be taken from qualified accounts by April of the year following the year in which you turn age 70½.

The tax savings for Harry and Matilda lowered the amount they needed to draw from their PRM from $90,000 to $65,000 (inflation adjusted with the $30,000 balance of the income need coming from Social Security) for as long as their tax-free distributions could last. We will consider the interest from the bank accounts sufficient to pay any income taxes due for those years. Other assumptions used are a 5 percent rate of return for the Roth IRA and a 6 percent return on the IRA. The annual income need will be inflated by just 2 percent given that Harry is a high-income earner, and there will be no spending habit change reductions in later segments of his financial freedom years. Social Security income increases by just $600 per year. Let's look at the following table to see the Safensound's distribution order under this scenario.

OPTIMAL DISTRIBUTION ORDER

	Soc. Sec.	Bank	Bank Balance	Roth IRA	Roth Bal.	IRA	IRA Bal.	Annual Income	Tax on SS	Total Tax
ROR			0%		5%		6%	2%		
Year			$175,000		$75,000		$1,345,000			
Year 1	$30,000	$50,000		0		$15,000		$95,000	0	
			$125,000		$78,750		$1,410,700			
Year 2	$30,600	$51,300		0		$15,000		$96,900	0	
			$73,700		$82,687		$1,496,242			
Year 3	$31,200	$52,638		0		$15,000		$98,838	0	
			$21,062		$86,821		$1,571,016			
Year 4	$31,800	$21,062		$32,952		$15,000		$100,814	0	
			0		$57,440		$1,650,227			
Year 5	$32,400	0		$55,431		$15,000		$102,831	0	
					$3,541		$1,734,294			
Year 6	$33,000	0		$3,541		$93,948		$130,489	$7,012	$30,499
					0		$1,743,146			
Year 7	$33,600	0		0		$101,539		$135,139	$7,162	$32,546
							$1,744,718		$14,174	$63,045

As you can see, by creating a distribution order in which we draw from after-tax assets first, we are able to reduce or eliminate taxes on Social Security income for an extended period. Not only would we draw from after-tax assets first, but we also draw from the lowest yielding and/or lowest net-after-tax yielding investments first. This results in a greater amount of money left in higher yielding investments for longer periods. The result is improved overall portfolio returns, as our highest yielding assets are able to grow by more than the amounts being withdrawn. Investments that are associated with higher returns are also those with higher risk of capital loss. Risk assets such as stock investments are long term in nature. It's advisable to maintain the flexibility not to draw down on stocks when the markets are doing poorly. Let's first look at the tax-planning aspects of distribution planning and then incorporate risk management into the equation.

Always remember that *it's not how much you make, it's how much you keep that matters.* So another very important factor in determining distribution order is which assets offer the best tax treatment for their earnings. The Roth IRA offers the best tax treatment, because earnings are tax exempt, meaning you will never have to pay tax on those earnings. The traditional IRA offers favored treatment where earnings are tax deferred, which means that you don't have to pay tax on them until you draw them out in the future. If you own stocks outside of an IRA in an after-tax account, dividend income and capital gains on the sale of stock are taxed at a lower rate than ordinary income. Those stocks that remain in your portfolio at death may be passed to your heirs free of taxation on any gains. Given that stocks present a higher degree of risk in hopes of providing the higher portfolio yields, we must also consider that they need to be held for longer periods to provide those expected returns.

Creating an optimal distribution order requires careful consideration for the taxation of Social Security benefits, your overall income tax bracket, the potential returns for each segment of your portfolio, and the time frame for the investments within your portfolio. Portfolio management during your distribution years also requires careful attention to the proper investment allocations. Investment allocation can and should vary by the potential use of the accounts in question.

For example, given that the first bucket was for short-term use, it required liquidity. This type of money would have to be invested conservatively in CDs and savings accounts, which would assure that the money was readily available without risk. As a result, that money would earn a very low after-tax rate of return. The money held in the Roth IRA could be invested for better yields, possibly in corporate bonds, because we knew we had several years before planning to access it, and it also offers us a tax exemption on returns. Even if the returns were the same at the bank as in the Roth IRA, a 5 percent tax-exempt yield is much better than a 5 percent taxable yield. The longer you can have money earning higher net after-tax yields, the more money you will have.

Your IRA could contain a significant allocation of high-growth investments such as stocks. This would make sense in part because we will need some degree of growth in our portfolio, and your IRA likely represents the largest portion of your PRM assets. These assets are intended to last for many years as a long-term investment.

It's true that both the IRA and the Roth IRA could be held for long-term use and provide tax-advantaged returns. However, the differentiator comes with the tax planning and understanding that while both IRAs offer tax-deferred returns, only the Roth IRA offers tax-exempt distributions.

Given their desired income level, the Safensounds would quickly jump to paying income tax on 85 percent of their Social Security benefit with as little as $30,000 of taxable income. Because the brackets for taxing Social Security benefits are relatively unforgiving, we chose to maximize the use of the bank and tax-exempt Roth IRA funds to meet their income needs for as long as possible to minimize the taxation of the Social Security benefits. Essentially, by using the after-tax bank account and Roth IRA for the first five years, while limiting taxable distributions from their IRA, they saved over $33,000 in taxes on their Social Security benefits alone.

While they were enjoying this tax relief, they were also enjoying *tax-deferred returns in their IRA, which were far greater than the taxable withdrawals.* This enabled the IRA to grow to an amount greater than the initial total asset value of the PRM and to continue growing up to seven years after they began taking income.

Let's look at a similar table where the income is taken from the bank and IRA sources without a plan for taxation or an optimal distribution order. For this example, we consider taking an equal amount of $15,000 per year from the bank account and the balance of the income need from the IRA. We will leave the Roth IRA to continue to accumulate earnings on a tax-exempt basis. The income need will initially be $115,000, as we do not have as much of the benefit of tax savings to reduce the $120,000 gross income need.

UNPLANNED DISTRIBUTION ORDER

	Soc. Sec.	Bank	Bank Balance	Roth IRA	Roth Bal.	IRA	IRA Bal.	Total	Tax on SS	Total Tax
ROR			0%		5%		6%	2%		
Year			$175,000		$75,000		$1,345,000			
2012	$30,000	$15,000		-		$70,000		$115,000	$6,375	$23,875
			$160,000		$78,750		$1,354,810			
2013	$30,600	$15,000		-		$71,700		$117,300	$6,502	$24,427
			$145,000		$82,687		$1,363,467			
2014	$31,200	$15,000		-		$73,446		$119,646	$6,630	$24,991
			$130,000		$86,821		$1,370,852			
2015	$31,800	$15,000		-		$75,239		$122,039	$6,757	$25,567
			$115,000		$91,162		$1,376,841			
2016	$32,400	$15,000		-		$77,080		$124,480	$6,885	$26,155
			$100,000		$95,720		$1,381,296			
2017	$33,000	$15,000		-		$78,969		$126,969	$7,012	$26,754
			$85,000		$100,506		$1,384,081			
2018	$33,600	$15,000		-		$80,908		$129,508	$7,162	$27,389
			$70,000		$105,531		$1,385,037		$47,323	4179,158

In the above example of an unplanned distribution order, you can see how much more in income tax is paid during the initial years of financial freedom. The result is that Harry and Matilda paid $47,323 in income taxes on their Social Security benefits over those seven years. This is $33,149 that they didn't have to pay in the optimal distribution order. What's worse is that because of their higher income tax burden, they needed to draw more taxable income each year to meet their need for $120,000 gross income. After seven years, they paid a total of $179,158 in income tax vs. only $63,045 in the optimal plan. Thus, the optimal plan saved them $116,113 in taxes over the first seven years of their financial freedom.

I'm sure the big question now is, are the Safensounds going to be able to rely on their PRM to produce the income they need for the rest of their life? As you recall, they started with approximately $200,000 less than what is needed by design for their PRM to produce their freedom income need. The table below picks up where the distribution order table left off. Harry would now be 73 and have more money than he started this journey with, at $1,744,718. The assumptions here are that the PRM portfolio earns a 5.5 percent rate of return, his income need is inflated by 2 percent, and there is no present value reduction of income needs based on changes in spending habits over time. The calculation is based on the amount needed to fund the PRM adequately from that point until Harry reaches 95, while also satisfying their income need. The amount required to accomplish this is $1,636,848, which is $107,870 less than what they have after the first seven years under the plan. That extra money can grow and be an inheritance for their children or grandchildren, be available to cover an emergency need in the family, or be there should the Safensounds live longer than expected and need to extend their PRM. The $107,870 accumulating at 5.5 percent annual returns will grow to in excess of $369,500 by the time Harry and Matilda reach age 95. This positive difference is a cushion that increases the reliability of their financial independence.

SAFENSOUND DISTRIBUTION SCHEDULE

From age 73, to spend 22 years in retirement
you'll need $1,636,848.53, if you:
earn an annual interest rate of 5.5 percent (compounded annually),
with an annual inflation rate of 2 percent,
and withdraw $103,641.00 (in 2013 dollars) at the beginning of each year.

Year	Beginning Balance	Withdrawal Amount	Earnings	Remaining
2013	$1,636,848.53	$103,641.00	$84,326.41	$1,617,533.94
2014	$1,617,533.94	$105,713.82	$83,150.11	$1,594,970.23
2015	$1,594,970.23	$107,828.10	$81,792.82	$1,568,934.95
2016	$1,568,934.95	$109,984.66	$80,242.27	$1,539,192.56
2017	$1,539,192.56	$112,184.35	$78,485.45	$1,505,493.66
2018	$1,505,493.66	$114,428.04	$76,508.61	$1,467,574.23
2019	$1,467,574.23	$116,716.60	$74,297.17	$1,425,154.80
2020	$1,425,154.80	$119,050.93	$71,835.71	$1,377,939.58
2021	$1,377,939.58	$121,431.95	$69,107.92	$1,325,615.55
2022	$1,325,615.55	$123,860.59	$66,096.52	$1,267,851.48
2023	$1,267,851.48	$126,337.80	$62,783.25	$1,204,296.93
2024	$1,204,296.93	$128,864.56	$59,148.78	$1,134,581.16
2025	$1,134,581.16	$131,441.85	$55,172.66	$1,058,311.97
2026	$1,058,311.97	$134,070.68	$50,833.27	$975,074.56
2027	$975,074.56	$136,752.10	$46,107.74	$884,430.19
2028	$884,430.19	$139,487.14	$40,971.87	$785,914.92
2029	$785,914.92	$142,276.88	$35,400.09	$679,038.13
2030	$679,038.13	$145,122.42	$29,365.36	$563,281.07
2031	$563,281.07	$148,024.87	$22,839.09	$438,095.30
2032	$438,095.30	$150,985.37	$15,791.05	$302,900.98
2033	$302,900.98	$154,005.07	$8,189.27	$157,085.18
2034	$157,085.18	$157,085.18	$.0	$.0
Totals		**$2,829,293.95**	**$1,192,445.43**	

The beneficial effect of an optimal distribution plan is substantial. As you can see with the story of the Safensounds, what initially appeared to be a shortfall in their PRM assets was turned into an excess through careful planning. That excess resulted from the reduction of income taxes over five to six years combined with the highest yielding investments working longer to build more wealth.

In the optimal distribution plan, the Safensounds had $1,744,718 remaining in their PRM after the seventh year of income and more than they needed to fund their PRM through age 95 based on the earnings estimates. With the unplanned method, they would have only $1,560,568, which would continue to represent a shortfall in the PRM. That's a difference of $184,150! The combination of tax savings and well-positioned assets earning compounded returns turned a shortfall into a surplus for the Safensounds in seven years. Proper distribution planning created an additional $184,150 of wealth for their family!

ACTION ITEM

Review your options to contribute to either a Roth IRA or Roth 401(k). Consider that although you may not be eligible for a tax-deductible IRA, you may be eligible to contribute to a Roth IRA, in addition to your 401(k).

For those readers who are not eligible to contribute to a Roth IRA or don't have additional savings compensation to put into a Roth IRA, consider diverting part of your 401(k) contributions to a Roth 401(k) account. If your employer does not offer Roth 401(k) provisions in your plan, request that they add it. Other than the cost to amend their plan, there is no reason an employer should refuse.

CREATING A RELIABLE INCOME STREAM FOR YOUR PRM

The choice of which investments to make in order to provide income for your financial freedom is as tantamount to your long-term success as your distribution order is to reducing your tax liability. Years before you declare financial independence, you should be *considering investment strategies that will create a reliable income for you during your financial freedom years.* This reliability of income (ROI) factor will be as important as your average rate of return in determining how long your assets will last. The less likely it is for your portfolio to experience sharp losses in market value and the more reliable the income sources in your portfolio, the more predictable the outcome.

To establish a high ROI factor in your PRM, you may need to incorporate a different investment style than what you would have used during your accumulation years. A strong ROI requires a high degree of predictability. In order to have predictability, you will need sources of guaranteed income. We know that cash equivalents like CDs can offer a guarantee not to lose principal, but the rate of return itself may be too low to invest more than a small portion of our PRM assets. We know that bonds provide a steady income. However, there is interest rate risk and other risks, so it's not a guarantee, but the income from bonds is reasonably predictable. Therefore, we can consider bonds as part of a reliable income strategy. However, it is critical to choose bond investments wisely given the current interest rate environment. We know that stocks that pay dividends may be a valuable part of your portfolio, but dividends and stock prices are far from predictable. One of the most commonly used investment products used to provide a source for predictable income is an annuity.

Some annuities are investment products such as mutual funds coupled with an insurance contract that offer a promise to pay income for a certain period of time to the holder of the contract. There are also fixed annuities, which are very similar to long-term CDs. Building annuities into your PRM is another way to increase your ROI. Provided your investment in annuities is made at the right time in your financial life and the amount allocated to annuities is in the appropriate proportion of your total PRM assets, these products may offer you a viable investment alternative for your PRM. You should consult a financial advisor for products like annuities and ask him/her to explain how they work and the differences between the various annuity products.

CREATING A BUCKET INVESTMENT STRATEGY

In the bucket strategy, we use CDs, short-term bonds, and savings accounts in Bucket 1 because we expected to spend down those assets in a relatively short term. They also represent the conservative component of our overall portfolio allocation.

However, in Bucket 2, our objective will be to earn a higher return of approximately 5 percent, which will require us to position less conservative investments in the portfolio. So in Bucket 2 we will seek those returns through intermediate-term corporate and government bonds, fixed annuities, and possibly some variable annuity investments.

In general, bonds are less volatile than stocks and provide a more reliable income than a typical stock fund or stock portfolio. Bond values will vary as interest rates rise and/or fall. Bonds are most attractive when interest rates are high and/or falling, and they are least attractive when interest rates are low and/or rising. A properly managed bond portfolio can provide a reasonable level of income that can be relied on. Given that bonds have relatively low volatility, bond positions can be liquidated when required to satisfy your income needs.

During the first ten years of your financial freedom, you would be advised to use Buckets 1 and 2 as your primary income source. Therefore, the assets in Bucket 3 generally will not be necessary to produce much income.

In Bucket 3, our investment objective is *long-term growth*.

Long-term growth is typically associated with investments in stock, real estate, or commodities. All of these have risk and require a longer-term outlook in order to have the best opportunity for successful performance. Thus, these are the type of investments you will likely want to use in Bucket 3.

Investing in dividend-paying stocks can be an attractive strategy for your equity investments. In fact, it's a tried and true strategy that many investors in their accumulation years will live by as a way to grow assets. For a person or family in their distribution years, dividend stocks when carefully selected can be a viable strategy for creating income that's fairly reliable. Dividend stocks become particularly attractive when interest rates are low, as the yields from these dividends can be greater than from certain bond investments.

To properly manage the risks associated with stocks of any kind, you must carefully allocate that portion of your portfolio, so that you will not need access to the principal for at least five to seven years. Taking the dividends as income, without selling the underlying stocks, to supplement your financial freedom needs is a great strategy to diversify your portfolio and develop another source of income. There are many great companies in the United States and around the world that have paid their shareholders increasing dividends for decades. However, it should be noted that dividends are not guaranteed and can be stopped at any time. In addition, the value of your stocks will fluctuate, which is why you must not be in a position where you need to sell those stocks during down markets.

The final step in creating a bucket strategy is to calculate how much money you need to allocate to the first two buckets given the rate of return they will receive and the number of years you wish to have them as the primary income source. Seek the assistance of a qualified financial advisor to assist you with these calculations.

The illustration below shows an example of a bucket strategy and the possible types of investments that you could consider for each bucket.

POSSIBLE OPTIMAL BUCKET STRATEGY ALLOCATION:

Assumes $1,000,000 PRM assets

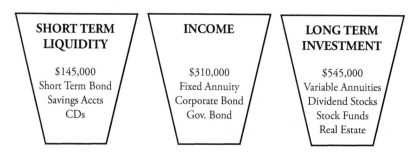

SHORT TERM LIQUIDITY	INCOME	LONG TERM INVESTMENT
$145,000	$310,000	$545,000
Short Term Bond	Fixed Annuity	Variable Annuities
Savings Accts	Corporate Bond	Dividend Stocks
CDs	Gov. Bond	Stock Funds
		Real Estate

The most important part of creating an optimal bucket strategy and a reliable income from your PRM is to first build the PRM to the appropriate amount needed for your financial freedom. From there you will find it comforting to know that you've accomplished something great. You and your family can enjoy your later years with true freedom and be free of financial stress, and you will have a number of investment options to consider for the next phase of your financial life. Each investor has different needs based on their personal risk tolerance and income goals. The examples given in this book are general in nature and should only be considered as a guide. Proper investment guidance requires detailed investigation and knowledge of your personal needs as well as the opportunities that may be suitable for you. Invest wisely, and carefully review your investment alternatives before investing.

ACTION STRATEGY

If you are in your accumulation years striving to achieve financial freedom, consider the value of tax-free distributions in your future. Refer to the Seven Rules for Successful Investing and note number 4. Use Roth contributions wisely. Develop a plan to divert a portion of your 401(k) contributions to Roth without lowering your total. Continue to put a substantial portion of your contributions in the Roth 401(k) option throughout your working years.

If you are approaching that time in your life when you will begin taking distributions from your PRM, review the different types of savings/investment accounts you have. Develop a plan to utilize the principal portion of your after-tax accounts to provide income. Always, draw from the lowest yielding after-tax account first. The next type of account in the distribution order would be your Roth IRA. If you have a Roth 401(k), keep in mind that this can easily be converted to a Roth IRA.

Determine your Social Security benefit and calculate the maximum amount of taxable (or attributable) income that you may receive before you would have to pay income tax on your Social Security benefits. Consider all types of income such as dividends and interest to determine how much you may draw from your taxable IRA. Continue to take the balance of your income need from the principal in banks and other after-tax accounts as long as they last. Once those assets are drawn down to near zero, proceed to draw from your Roth accounts to avoid crossing the threshold into taxation of your Social Security benefits for as long as possible.

Seek the assistance of a financial advisor to create your own bucket strategy for proper investment and income allocations.

HOW NICE

I'm sure many of my readers are looking forward to the day when they have built wealth similar to the Safensound's and can declare financial independence.

How nice that will be!

But the fact is, we can all make the choice to achieve this level of success. Remember that all the numbers are relative to your lifestyle, and your lifestyle is relative to your income. Do not be concerned if you have more or less than someone else but rather that you have determined your dream for financial freedom and taken all of the steps toward reaching that dream. Rejoice in what you have. Enjoy your life today and plan for the future. Do not compromise one for the other but rather live within your means and avoid excesses and costly financial mistakes.

There are many things that can happen to us as we journey through life, many of which are far more important than money. Your self-esteem and character will be built by the way in which you conduct yourself and the way you care for the people in your life, not by how much money you have. Opportunities will present themselves to those who are committed to success and to doing what is right.

The following is one of my favorite quotes and a fundamental belief that I live by:

> "Concerning all acts of initiative (and creation), there is one elementary truth... The moment one definitely commits oneself, then providence moves too. All sorts of things occur to help one that would never otherwise have occurred. A whole stream of events issues from the decision, raising in one's favor all manner of unforeseen

incidents, meetings and material assistance which no man could have dreamt would have come his way. I have learned a deep respect for one of Geothe's couplets:

Whatever you can do, or dream you can, begin it. Boldness has genius, power, and magic in it."

—W.H. Murray

Your 401(k) plan or employer-sponsored retirement plan is one of your most valuable resources in the process of creating wealth. The federal government wants you to succeed, and they provide you with substantial tax advantages to help you along the way. All of the tools you will need are in place for you to accomplish your objective. If you truly wish to declare financial independence, consider implementing the strategies discussed in this book as soon as possible. Keep in mind that one of the most important factors in determining your success is your level of commitment to achieving your goals.

I wish all of my readers good fortune, good health, and happiness throughout your life.

And … "May your children have rich parents!"

WEALTH ACCUMULATION CHEAT SHEET

"While there may be many emotions such as pride and ego that will influence how we use our money, it is critical that we balance those emotional needs with our true, long-term financial needs." —*page 18*

"The greater the financial commitment, the more important it is that you stay within your financial means." —*page 20*

"The earliest dollars saved are the most valuable retirement income producers." —*page 25*

Financial Freedom: "The ability to do the things you enjoy doing while living the lifestyle you prefer and having the freedom to do that without concern for money."—*page 39*

"The cost of procrastination is far greater than the price of sacrifice." —*page 32*

"I have yet to meet anyone who wouldn't want a Personal Retirement Machine, just a lot of people who aren't sure how to get one." —*page 33*

"Sacrifice is the intelligence to know the value of allocating resources toward the achievement of a future goal, as opposed to expending them for short-term gratification." —*page 37*

"Free cash flow is the money that flows into your pockets but doesn't flow out in a given period, and it's from free cash flow that wealth is created. By clearing the way for free cash flow through debt reduction and spending controls, you may then invest that free cash into the building blocks of your financial future." —*page 32*

Follow these Seven Rules for Successful 401k Investing

1. Be Patient. Patience comes to those who wait.

2. Use dollar cost averaging, and never stop contributing.

3. Take advantage of Uncle Sam's interest-free loans.

4. Use Roth contributions wisely.

5. Diversify, diversify, diversify, and rebalance.

6. Invest a percentage of salary, not a flat dollar amount.

7. Never take withdrawals.

—*page 93*

"You've got to have money to make money." —*page 138*

"If you want a portfolio that will always have investments in the top-performing market sectors, you should allocate investments to all of them." —*page 143, 155*

"The next step in portfolio management, once you've established the right asset allocation, is to rebalance your portfolio annually." —*page 154*

"Dollar cost averaging, asset allocation, and rebalancing are the tools that should enable you to have the confidence to spend time in the market and avoid market timing mistakes." —*page 154*

"To be truly diversified, your portfolio must also hold investments that are not directly correlated to stock market performance, such as real estate and commodities." —*page 159*

"One of the most potentially damaging things an investor can do to his/her portfolio is to attempt to time the market." —*page 160*

"A good rule of thumb is that your PRM will cost twenty times your financial freedom income number or ten times your pre-freedom income." —*page 121*

"When rates are high, stocks will die. When rates are low, stocks will grow." —*page 177*

"If you can make significant contributions to a Roth 401(k) account on a consistent basis, you will be rewarded during your distribution years." —*page 253*

"Taking an early withdrawal from your 401k plan or IRA is like paying back Uncle Sam's interest-free loan early." —*page 233*

"It's not how much you make, it's how much you keep that matters." —*page 256*

Ipswich Bay Advisors is an award-winning wealth management and financial services organization. We provide a broad set of solutions for corporations, their valued employees, and high-net-worth individuals. We take the time to get to know our clients and employ some of the most advanced research and financial planning systems to help them achieve their goals. Ipswich Bay Advisors is an affiliate of The Capital Advisory Group, LLC of Bloomington, MN.

Our Mission

Through our commitment to excellence, caring and the highest level of customer service, we continuously seek that which is in the best interest of each client respectively, providing innovative business and wealth management strategies and insight into the opportunities for financial growth.

Please visit us at

www.ipswichfinancial.com.

Ipswich Bay Advisors, 150A Andover Street, Suite 2, Danvers, MA 01923
Capital Advisory Group Advisory Services, LLC / Investors Capital Corporation
p. 877.777.6554 / f. 978.777.6560

Printed in the USA
CPSIA information can be obtained
at www.ICGtesting.com
JSHW012022140824
68134JS00033B/2821

9 781599 326801